Minor Complications

Two plays by Brendan Gall

Coach House Books, Toronto

First edition

For production enquiries, please contact singlethreatproductions@gmail.com

  Canadä

Published with the generous assistance of the Canada Council for the Arts and the Ontario Arts Council. Coach House Books also gratefully acknowledges the support of the Government of Ontario through the Ontario Book Publishing Tax Credit and the Government of Canada through the Canada Book Fund.

The Playwright gratefully acknowledges the financial assistance of Tarragon Theatre, the Canada Council for the Arts and the 2009 Banff Playwrights Colony, a partnership between the Canada Council for the Arts, the Banff Centre and Alberta Theatre Projects.

LIBRARY AND ARCHIVES CANADA CATALOGUING IN PUBLICATION

Gall, Brendan
    Minor complications : two plays / by Brendan Gall.

Contents: A quiet place -- Wide awake hearts.
ISBN 978-1-55245-237-0

    I. Title.

PS8613.A459285M44 2010   C812'.6   C2010-907051-8

Wide Awake Hearts

a nightmare with no intermission

This is for you.

Wide Awake Hearts was produced by Tarragon Theatre under the artistic direction of Richard Rose. It premiered on November 10, 2010, with the following cast and creative team:

A: Gord Rand
B: Lesley Faulkner
C: Raoul Bhaneja
D: Maev Beaty

Direction: Gina Wilkinson
Assistant Direction: Kristina Nicoll
Script Coordination: Nathaniel Bryan
Sex and Violence Direction: John Stead
Stage Management: Beatrice Campbell

Production Design: Lorenzo Savoini
Lighting Design: Bonnie Beecher
Composition and Sound Design: Mike Ross

Production Management: Michael Freeman
Technical Direction: Paul Fujimoto
Head Carpenter: Ian Chappell
Head Scenic Artist: Lindsay Anne Black
Wardrobe: Michelle Bailey
Props: Lokki Ma
Theatre Technician: Kevin Hutson

Playwright's Note

Characters are hard and dry, until they aren't. Sounds are unsettling. Lighting is low-key. Sets are spare, waiting in the shadows like stored museum pieces. Use of a forward slash within a character's dialogue indicates the point of overlap where the following character begins to speak. 'Shifts' occur in the blink of an eye – transitioning characters ripped away before they are ready, the end of the last scene bleeding into the next.

Wide Awake Hearts *could not have been written without the help of a great number of people; the playwright wishes to express heartfelt thanks to Aaron Abrams, Chad Donella, Martin Gero, Andrea Romaldi, Richard Rose, Vicki Stroich and Gina Wilkinson for their invaluable feedback on various drafts; actors Graham Abbey, Aaron Abrams, David Beazely, Caroline Cave, Diana Donnelly, Matthew Edison, Tracey Ferencz, Fabrizio Filippo, Michelle Giroux, Jonathan Goad, Kate Hewlett, Jamie Konchak, Trevor Leigh, Mary Long, Brendan Murray, Paul Rainville and Amy Rutherford for lending their voices to A, B, C or D at various stages in the process; to everyone at Tarragon Theatre, and, of course, to the fearless cast and creative team of the first production – I cannot thank you enough. To Alana Wilcox and everyone at Coach House Books. And, finally, to KK – all the rest of the letters in my alphabet.*

Wide Awake Hearts

Darkness. Opening credits. The climax of a requiem.

Title card: WIDE AWAKE HEARTS

The curtain rises to reveal B and C standing, locked in a passionate kiss, A sitting on the couch behind them, silently talking as he works on opening a bottle of red wine, seemingly unaware of them. B and C part and sit on separate pieces of furniture – B next to A, C facing them – as the music stops.

A: … The whole thing's a nightmare. This one today – they go through the blocking with him, they rehearse, he *acts* like he understands – nods and smiles and hugs Mommy's leg – and then they go to *shoot* and all of a sudden he's wandering off his mark to go play with some cigarette lighter that's not even in frame. I mean he was literally sending Continuity into panic attacks. Finally the director gets down in front of him, you know, down to his level like the books say you're supposed to, looks him right in the eye and says, 'Sunshine? You're acting like a little four-year-old kid right now.' And all right, yes, he *is* a little four-year-old kid, granted, but we're paying him to *look* like a four-year-old kid, not *behave* like one. This child was nothing but grace and dignity in the read-through – he was a goddamn paragon of professionalism, so you know he's capable of it. But then he gets on set and all of a sudden it's Mardi Gras. That's why you *always* cast a spare, in case you have to switch them out. And I swear to god, we were right on the verge. And Kid B could smell it …

He pours a splash of wine into his glass and swirls it around.

Like a little baby shark tasting blood in the water …

He tastes the wine before filling their glasses.

It's funny too, because Kid A and Kid B inevitably end up playing together, and it's always this weird dynamic where, I mean of *course* they're gonna play together, they're kids, but there's also this weird little manipulation dance going on just below the surface …

A rubs B's leg absently as he talks.

I mean your Kid A's are generally pretty oblivious. They think the part's a lock, their guard's down. I guess they figure this other kid's just some hired play-buddy for their amusement or something. But your Kid B's always stay frosty. Their play is always just a little more pointed, a little more for the benefit of the grown-ups in the room, like, 'Hey, look how much cuter *I* play. Look how beautifully unaware and innocent my *play* is.' Or sometimes it's about outright sabotage. This backup today, he spent the whole morning trying to make Kid A play word games with him between setups. I couldn't figure it out. Then I realize: *Kid B's running a grift*, trying to make him forget his lines! You gotta respect that, I mean that is smart. Anyway, suffice it to say tensions are running way past high. Kid A's halfway out the door and everyone knows it but him. His work's sloppy in the master, he's all over the place in coverage, paraphrasing, dropping lines, flubbing takes. The director keeps looking over at me like, *Is this really happening? Are we gonna do this? Are we really gonna pull the plug on this kid?* Because it is now or it is never, the time has come for all good men to come to the aid of their party, I've got my finger on the button … And *then* we go in for *his* coverage, and all of a sudden he just … *turns it on. Kills it.* Hits his mark, bats his eyelashes, nails his dialogue and lights up the punchline like a goddamn Christmas tree. The little brat was *saving it for his close-up*. Finally, he finishes the take, this endless, *perfect* take ... There's this long silence ... The director finally manages to whisper, '*Cut* ... ' And the whole crew *explodes* into applause. I've never seen anything like it. You shoulda seen Kid B's face: no joy in Mudville. There is no Santa Claus. The Tooth Fairy murdered the Easter Bunny. Turns out: the world doesn't need you.

Beat.

We were *this close* to having to scrap the whole day. We can't *afford* to scrap a whole day ... And then this *kid* just ... I swear to god, the whole thing's a nightmare.

Beat.

Upshot is, I think it's gonna make a hell of an opening scene. Kid A set it up; you two can't knock it down it's your own damn fault.

He drinks.

Anyway.

A raises his glass.

To the dream factory.

B and C raise their glasses.

B & C: To the dream factory.

They drink.

A: How was your flight.

C: I don't know, I slept through it.

A: But it was all right.

C: Yeah, I guess. Middle seat. (*smiling at A*) The producer must be a real cheapskate.

A: (*smiling back*) Independent filmmaking: no corner left uncut.

B: How is it out there?

C: Pretty dead right now. But the air's cleaner.

B: Mountains, ocean …

C: That's the rumour.

A: I never did understand why you left like that. One day I just woke up … and you were gone. You could've owned this town.

C: Yeah, well. Why buy when you can rent.

    Beat.

I guess I just needed a change of scenery.

A: What's wrong with our scenery.

C: Nothing. I just had to stop looking at it.

    Silence.

Hey, thanks again for making this happen. I know you really had to push for me.

A: No one wants to listen to the writer. Even when he's the producer. In the end I just told them the part was written for you. It's the role you were born to play.

C: How am I supposed to take that.

A: In the spirit in which it was given.

B: He means it as a compliment.

A: There's no shame in playing to your strength.

C: And what's that.

A: Your weakness of character.

C: Gee, thanks.

A: Nice people make dull drama.

C: I'd kill to play nice.

A: I'll see what I can do.

C: What's the deal anyway, I thought I heard you were done with features.

A: Well, I guess they weren't done with me. Call it my swan song.

   Beat.

B: Well, I'm looking forward to it. I finally get to play someone who doesn't need rescuing.

C: Least one of us gets to stretch.

B: Gee, thanks.

A: I've missed this. When's the last time we were all in the same room together.

   Silence.

   It's good to see you.

C: Why don't I believe that.

B: It's his poker face. He has very few tells.

C: I used to be able to read him like a book.

A: Lucky for me you don't read books.

C: No, but I like to look at the pictures.

A: Me too.

B: Where are they putting you up?

C: Super 8. Out by the airport.

B: You're kidding. How did *that* happen?

C: Maybe they figure it's good for the character.

A: That must be it.

B: More like good for their pocketbooks.

A: Call it research.

B: I call it cheap. You should be putting him somewhere halfway decent.

A: Hey, we can put him at the Park Hyatt if you don't mind shooting without film in the camera.

C: We're shooting on film?

A: Figure of speech.

B: He should stay here.

    Silence.

C: I'm … not sure that's such a great idea.

A: Me neither.

B: Why not?

    Beat.

He's your oldest friend.

A: That doesn't mean I like him.

B: When's the last time we've seen each other.

A: We're seeing each other right now.

B: We have an empty room. It just sits there.

A: That's my office.

B: You write in the attic.

A: I *think* in the attic; I write in the *basement*.

B: The room's empty. It just sits there.

A: So you've mentioned.

C: I'm fine where I am.

A: See? The man could sleep on a park bench.

C: Actually, I have slept on a park bench.

B: That doesn't mean he should.

C: Who cares where I'm sleeping, I'll be asleep.

A: Well said.

B: You're being ridiculous.

A: *You're* being ridiculous.

B: He should sleep here.

C: I'm fine where I am.

A: See? He's fine where he is.

B: All right, fine, then I guess we're all fine. I give up, sleep with the roaches.

Silence.

A: Hey … You know what you should *do* … You should stay *here*.

Silence.

The Super 8 was a joke. I just wanted to see if you'd say anything.

C: Oh.

Beat.

Good one.

A: We shoot for a month – you really thought I was going to make you sleep in a Bukowski novel?

C: I've slept in worse.

A: I always meant for you to stay here.

Silence.

What, you don't enjoy our company?

C: No, it's just. The script is. There's just. A lot of. Things to keep track of. A lot of words.

A: It's true, I even use some of them twice.

C: But just. In terms of the story. There's a lot of. Things going on, and. Some of it's pretty …

A: Subtle. Thank you. Yes.

C: I just. Want to make sure I stay on top of everything. You know. Do my homework. I wanna do this right. If I stayed here, I just.

It would be easy to let myself ... Don't get me wrong, it's great to see you, but. I just. I don't want to confuse business with pleasure.

A: What if we promise not to be pleasant.

Silence.

C: I wouldn't be imposing.

B: Don't be stupid.

A: Yeah, don't be *stupid*.

Beat.

You're my oldest friend.

Beat.

When's the last time we've seen each other.

Beat.

Like the lady said: We have an empty room.

Beat.

It just sits there.

Silence.

C: It's your party.

A: That's right. It is.

Beat.

It'll be fun. We can get up and do yoga together. You two can run lines.

Beat.

B: Good. Then it's settled.

> *She raises her glass.*

To old friends.

> *C raises his glass.*

C: To old friends.

B: And new endeavours.

> *A raises his glass.*

A: And new endeavours.

> *They drink.*

That's not half-bad, is it.

C: Yeah. Good legs.

A: 'Good legs.' You a connoisseur now.

C: Just a tourist.

A: Still the mysterious drifter, wandering through the wilderness.

C: So they tell me.

A: How much you think this bottle cost.

C: A thousand dollars.

A: Seven ninety-five. Her choice. She likes to slum.

B: I like what I like.

A: I don't know anyone who doesn't.

C: Good is good.

A: 'Good is good.' That is so true, good *is* good.

B: You're being a jerk.

A: Am I?

B: Yes. You're drunk.

A: Oh. Sorry. Red wine makes me a bit of a vampire.

C: I remember.

A: I just need something in my stomach. Is dinner ready.

B: Sure, if you don't mind blood.

A: Are you kidding, I love blood. You hungry.

C: Starving.

A: You good with blood.

C: Always.

A: 'Good.'

> *A stands.*

Then let's eat.

> *SHIFT.*

Sorry I'm late.

> *A is alone, the shade from a venetian blind casting him in strips of light and dark. He washes some pills down with a glass of water as he speaks, smiling and confident through most of the following.*

Choose your favourite excuse: Traffic. Parking. Locusts. Also, I think my wife and my best friend are fucking each other. Anyway. Not your concern. Not what this meeting is about.

Since I kept you all waiting, I'll cut to the chase: I can see from your faces that you've all read the one-sheet. Most of you, anyway. Some of you. Or maybe one of you read it and then explained it to everyone else. Regardless, clearly you all think it's shit. And you're right, it is shit. I mean it's not terrible, but it's not good either, which is just another polite way of saying it's shit. And the saddest part is, it's entirely produceable shit. Which is not to say I think you should produce it. Far from it. But we all know that there's a hell of a lot worse out there making money faster than a goddamn printing press. Is anyone familiar with the printing press? It's a tool they used to use to make something called a book. I read one once. It was all *right*.

Look, it's probably obvious by now that I'm not really prepared for this little get-together this morning. I'm not going to dazzle you. I won't be juggling or making balloon animals. I have no soft-shoe prepared. And the truth is, I really don't care. I have more than enough money. If I don't make another cent for the rest of my life, I will be more than comfortable. So listen to me as you would the last words of a dying man who has absolutely nothing to lose. Because I don't. I really don't.

We are, all of us, dying. Every day. This industry, I feel, is accelerating that process unnecessarily. We are grubs. Feeding on ourselves. Devouring ourselves from the inside out. That's just one metaphor, it's possible I'm having some sort of breakdown. *Now*: here's the radical thought I had on the drive in this morning while I was trying not to picture my best friend and my wife having sexual intercourse in my bed, her hand in his hair, my pillow under her back: drama. Is conflict. Right? Okay: *why is that*. What is it about us that makes us want to introduce more conflict into our already conflicted lives?

When my father watches television now, he falls asleep as soon as anyone starts yelling or shooting at each other. His nervous system can't take it, so he just shuts down. The man spent forty years spitting blood on the trading floor, now he can't handle the stress of prime-time TV, he has to literally fall asleep just to get away from it. You know what he likes now? The boring parts. The parts before everything gets fucked up. The filler.

What are we doing. Our life is conflict; peace and happiness should be our escape. Why is every other show on television about murder. We are, all of us, killing ourselves. What is so inherently *wrong with us*.

So forget the one-sheet, forget it. Shred it, recycle it, set it on fire – it'd sell enough Pepsi to run Niagara Falls, but forget it. Here's my new pitch, and I'm warning you now, you get the first shot at it, and it's only gonna come around once:

I'm going to write the first television drama in history ... with absolutely *no conflict*.

None.

Zero.

I'm thinking kind of a kaleidoscope-mosaic thing. There's this family. And they really love each other. And things are going pretty well for them. We watch them eat breakfast, and breakfast is delicious. They go off to work and school, and it's all pretty rewarding. And then they all come home and tell each other about it. And when one of them talks, the rest of them really listen, they really care what that person has to say. At night, they go to sleep and dream sweet dreams.

It's also about this young couple. And they're really in love. And we just sort of ... follow them around while they do things together: go to the movies, go for walks, kiss, make love, talk about the future. And we can see that they're really good for each other. We can tell that they're gonna make it.

It's also about this guy who loves his job. But he's not a workaholic; he's got a good balance going. It's a rewarding job, but it allows him to be creative without devouring him whole. Imagine that. *Imagine that if you are capable.* And on the weekends, get this: *he goes to the cottage with his dog.* He sits on the dock, throws sticks in the water and nurses an ice-cold bottle of beer. Never more than three. He is sublimely happy.

We want to know these people. We want to *be* these people. Because they are happy. We don't want anything bad to ever happen to them, and the beautiful thing is, we know that nothing ever will. And that's why we'll keep tuning in. Because we'll know that once every week, if only for an hour, we don't have to worry. Everything will be taken care of. Everyone will be safe.

It's so simple and perfect, I don't know why no one's ever thought of it before.

I can see by your faces that you all think I've lost it – I haven't.

Look, we all know that I could have sold you this regurgitated cop-show dreck if I'd really wanted to. I've done it before. I'm good at it. If I'd wanted to, I bet I could have convinced a hell of a lot of you that this terrible, *terrible* idea would make a really neat teevee show.

Most of you, anyway.

Some of you.

You. I bet I could have convinced you. Look at you, you're eating a prune danish, how old are you, kid, a thousand? You still kinda think it's a good idea, don't you. In your heart? It's okay, you're young; I'll be dead soon. They'll cut me into pieces and serve me at things like this. In a year you'll be dunking me in your coffee, it's okay. I'm okay with that. I'm almost thirty, I've had a good run. This business is for the young. I'm out of touch. I remember when there was no internet. True story. We had to use fax machines. In the snow. I'll be all right. I'm a dinosaur and you're a meteor, but I'll be okay. My brain's the size of a walnut. It's practically vestigial. I'll be fine, don't worry about me – *my father could have bench-pressed you*. He didn't even know how to read. Now he can't even watch TV. What's he supposed to do? It's none of your concern. What are *any of us* supposed to *do*.

It's possible I'm having some kind of breakdown. I'm going to go now, I have no idea where. I'll be all right.

Oh: just a sidebar. I'm not going to be coming to any more of these little circle jerks. You want to find me, you know where I live. Merry Christmas. Sorry I wasted your time.

B: Do you have any idea what *time* it is.

    SHIFT.

A: Hm?

B: Are you drunk.

A: I can't tell.

    Silence.

B: What news, my lord.

A: Hm?

B: How was your day.

A: … Interesting.

    Beat.

I think I sold a show.

B: Really? Which one?

A: The cop one. With an option on … something else.

B: *Really.*

A: Yeah. I think I found a new way to pitch.

B: Left-handed?

A: No-handed. With my eyes closed. Facing the wrong way.

B: Doesn't sound like you.

A: It doesn't?

>   *Silence.*

B: I thought you said you were done with television. You're done
    with television, you're done with movies …

A: I say a lot of things … Maybe I'm just done.

>   *Silence.*

B: You really sold the *cop show?*

A: Yeah.

B: *Really.*

A: You keep saying that – you don't like the cop show?

B: No, it's just –

A: A piece a shit?

B: That's not what I was going to say – please don't put words in
    my mouth.

A: Oh. Sorry. What were you going to say. 'It's just …' What.

>   *Beat.*

Derivative? Formulaic? *Safe?* Sorry, I'm doing it again.

B: Is something wrong.

Beat.

A: Did you kiss my best and oldest friend today.

Silence.

B: Yeah.

Silence.

A: How'd it go.

B: Fine. We got your changes for the ending. They're good. He finally tells her the truth.

A: Doesn't do them much good, though.

B: At least he's honest with her.

A: Thought I'd give him something new to play. But it went all right?

B: Yeah, I guess. I don't know. It was weird. Those things are *always* weird.

A: What things.

She looks at him.

Oh. Right.

Beat.

Yeah, I wanted to be there but … the day kind of got away from me.

B: No. I'm glad you weren't there. It was bad enough without you spying on us through the monitor, listening in on headset from the next room.

A: Right.

B: Is something wrong.

A: I don't know. I've had kind of a strange day.

B: Me too.

Silence.

B: You really sold the cop show?

Beat.

A: Yup.

B: Shouldn't we celebrate.

A: How would we do that.

Silence. She gives him a kiss. He looks at her. He kisses her deeply, moving them backward, pushing them down onto the couch.

(*still kissing*) I love you …

He moves down to her neck … her chest … her stomach, pushing up her shirt … She grows still. He moves up to her mouth again, but she's less responsive.

What.

B: Nothing, I just …

Beat.

I've sort of been doing this all day.

Beat. He sits up. Silence.

A: How is he.

Beat.

Is he a good kisser.

B: What are you doing.

A: Nothing. I'm just –

B: You brought him here. You hired him. You hired both of us.

A: I know that.

B: And now you're, what, trying to make me feel guilty about it.

A: It was just a question.

B: No. It wasn't. This was not my decision.

A: You didn't say no.

    Silence. B stares at A.

What.

B: How much of us is in this.

A: In what.

B: This movie. How invested are we. How much have we put up.

    Silence.

A: All of it. We're all in.

    Silence.

B: I wish … I wish I knew what you were doing.

    Beat.

A: I guess you'll just have to trust me.

Beat.

B: And what if it doesn't work. What happens to us then.

Beat.

A: Then we are truly fucked.

Silence.

So is he?

B: Is he *what.*

He looks at her.

What do you want me to say.

Beat.

He's incredible. Better than you'll ever be. He's exciting and dangerous, and you're boring and safe. He's everything you're not. I'm leaving you for him. We're running away together.

Beat.

Grow up.

Beat.

You made this world, the rest of us are just trying to live in it. I am trying to get through this. Do my job, play my part, whatever that is. What is *wrong with you.*

Beat.

He kisses her violently, pushing her back down on the couch. She resists for a moment, then reciprocates. A few passionate moments. He slides his hand underneath her shirt. Something starts to ring. Once. Twice. Three times.

(*still kissing*) It'll stop.

    Four.

A: (*still kissing*) What'll stop.

    Five. He stops and looks at her. Six.

What'll stop.

    Seven. She starts kissing him again. Eight. Nine. Ten. He stops again.

What's wrong.

    Eleven. He sits up and moves to the end of the bed. Twelve. B sits up. Thirteen. Fourteen. Fifteen. Sixteen. Silence.

A: You taste like cigarettes.

    His PDA vibrates in his pocket. He checks it.

B: What is it.

A: Production. We're firing the editor.

    Beat.

I have to go back in.

    He exits.

B: (*standing*) Please don't leave me alone right now.

    C kisses her neck from behind.

C: Let's pretend we're alone …

    SHIFT.

B: We are alone …

C: (*his arms around her*) Good, that'll make it easy …

B: What if he comes back …

C: (*his hands under her shirt*) There's no one here but us …

B: In the house?

C: (*turning her around*) In the world …

> *Breathless, they kiss and grope and undress each other throughout: standing, kneeling, against walls, on furniture, the floor, moving through the whole space, exhausting the options almost ridiculously …*

B: Everyone thinks they're the main character …

C: Yeah, but in my case it's actually true …

B: Someone has to play the supporting role …

C: Long as it's not me …

B: You're a real team player …

C: I prefer individual sports …

B: Tell me a story …

C: I love you …

B: That's original …

C: I also hate your guts …

B: Sounds complicated …

C: It is, I wanna kiss you and punch you at the same time …

B: You can't even walk and chew gum …

C: I'm a quick study …

B: Maybe you should slow down …

C: I want to tell you something … I've never loved anyone … Ever … I've never had my heart broken … I've never begged someone to stay … Or missed them when they were gone … I've never once had the thought, *I can't live without you* … Because the truth is … I can live without anyone …

B: You really need to work on your pillow talk …

C: I just hope I'm not a sociopath …

B: Can sociopaths hope …

C: I hope not …

B: Hey, I think you're cured …

C: I just wanted you to know that before we started …

B: We haven't started yet?

C: So we both know where we stand …

B: We're not even sitting …

C: I think it's important to be honest …

B: Oh my god, you are a sociopath …

C: I love the way you talk …

B: You should listen more closely …

C: I wanna marry you …

B: I think you got the wrong verb …

C: I wanna bear your children …

B: Pretty sure I have to do that part …

C: I wanna spend every second of every day of the rest of my life with you …

B: That's it?

C: I wanna grow old and die in your arms …

B: Sure, but what about the future …

C: I love you … And I've never loved anyone … Ever … I love you … I'm sorry … I love you … I think it's important you know that … Because I've never loved anyone … I love you … I can't live without you … It's possible I'm a sociopath … I love you …

B: I don't even know who you are …

C: I'm your guardian angel …

B: Then where's your halo …

C: It gave me a rash. Make love to me …

B: I don't even like you …

C: Don't get hung up on details. Let's make love …

B: Stop talking …

C: You're right, we transcend language …

B: No, you just sound like a moron …

C: I love your sense of humour …

B: And I thought it was my body …

C: That too …

B: A Renaissance man …

C: What do you like about *me* …

B: Your proximity …

C: Tell me what you want me to do …

B: Shut up …

C: After that …

B: That's the whole thing …

C: There's that sense of humour again …

B: Oh yeah, I see what you mean …

C: What do you want me to do to you …

B: Make me forget how dumb you are …

C: You don't mean that …

B: I don't mean a lotta things …

C: Sometimes when I look at you, I just wanna have you, right there on the floor …

B: It's good to have dreams …

C: And then other times I just wanna –

B: (*stopping*) Shh! Do you hear that?

> *They stop and listen. Beat.*

(*smiling*) Me neither.

> *She kisses him again. They start to tear off each other's clothes. It becomes less frantic, more intimate. They stop, staring into each other's eyes. Beat. A buzzer sounds. They continue to stare for a moment before she breaks away from him.*

C: (*out*) Okay.

He gets up and reaches for his clothes.

B: You can't.

He looks at her.

Continuity.

He considers this. They get up and sit next to each other on canvas director's chairs, half-naked. She reads a magazine. Silence.

C: This is a weird job sometimes.

Silence.

Why do you think he did this?

Silence.

B: I don't know. I guess he trusts you.

Silence.

C: Does he trust you?

Silence.

You don't think it's a little weird?

B: You didn't say no.

C: I'm not stupid.

She looks at him. Then back to her magazine.

I guess I was cheaper than getting a name.

She looks back at him. Then back to her magazine again.

What.

Beat.

What.

She looks back again.

B: He almost lost the film fighting to get you this. They threatened to kick him off his own movie.

Beat.

C: I didn't ask him to do that. You think this is fun for me?

B: Then why are you here.

Silence. She goes back to her magazine.

C: I'm not exactly in a position to turn down work. Anyway, it's a good script. He's a good writer. You're a good actor.

Beat.

Hey. Look at me.

She looks at him.

You're a good actor.

Beat. She goes back to her magazine.

B: Thank you.

C: You're welcome.

Silence.

Do you ever worry he only casts you because you're his wife.

B: No, I'd never thought of that.

Silence.

No.

Beat.

I know he does.

C: But you don't say no.

B: I'm not stupid.

C: Compared to what.

B: Compared to you, for starters.

C: Well, that's not saying much.

Silence.

What's taking them so long.

B: They're probably watching playback.

C: Yeah, I bet they are.

Silence.

We're gonna have to do it again, aren't we.

Beat.

And again. And again. And again …

Silence.

I like your outfit.

Silence.

Remember that night we found him on the front step. Carrying him upstairs, getting him into bed. Trying to get the knots out of his laces … But we couldn't. In the end we just left him there. Dead asleep. Snoring with his shoes still on.

Silence.

B: (*still reading*) He still does that sometimes.

C: Does he still tell you how beautiful you are every fifteen minutes.

Silence.

I used to be able to set my watch by it.

B: You didn't wear a watch.

C: I didn't need to.

Silence.

It's good to see you.

Beat.

You look great.

Silence.

'Thank you.'

Silence.

B: Thank you.

Beat.

You look like a car accident.

C: I'm in love with my best friend's wife, how am I supposed to look.

B: (*sharply*) What are you doing.

C: I don't know, what am I doing.

B: (*exiting*) I'm getting a water, you want anything.

C: Gum, if they have any.

B: (*off*) Good, you taste like an ashtray. I thought you said you quit.

C: I haven't even started.

> *Beat.*

> (*calling after*) Don't tell Mom and Dad.

> *Beat. He crouches down and looks under the couch for a sock.*

D: What are you doing.

> *A and D stand, watching him.*

> *SHIFT.*

A: Oh, sorry, this is –

> *C slumps into the couch to put on his sock, getting dressed as they talk.*

D: You look like a car accident.

> *Beat.*

C: It's for the role.

D: What, are you playing yourself.

C: I'm experimenting with Method.

D: That'd be a first.

C: What are you doing here.

D: I missed you too.

A: Sorry, do you two know each other?

D: You can't at least comb your hair.

C: I became an actor so I *wouldn't* have to comb my hair.

D: I thought you wanted to hold the mirror up to nature.

C: Nope, it was the comb thing. I take it you two have met.

D: Only in person.

A: Just now, at the door. I thought she was an actor.

D: I told him I was a human being.

C: She loves that joke.

D: (*to* C) Turns out I'm the new editor.

> *Silence.*

C: Of course you are. Small world.

D: Actually, it's an enormous world. With seven billion people living on it.

A: … And I am getting the distinct sense that you are also –

D: Yes. I am. Turns out it's possible to be more than one thing. I take it Brando here didn't mention he was seeing a lowly cutter.

A: Actually, he didn't mention you at all.

> *Beat.*

At least, I don't –
I mean, you know I'm sure he mentioned –
I've just, I've been so preoccupied / with –

D: You have a lovely home.

> *Beat.*

A: Thank you.

D: (*to* C) Have you been drinking.

C: What's with the past tense.

A: Can I get you one?

D: What's with the singular.

> *A exits. Silence.*

C: Least I'm not smoking.

D: What do you want, a ribbon.

C: I dunno, can you smoke ribbons.

> *A returns and hands her a glass of red wine.*

A: Here you go.

D: Thanks.

> *She throws it in C's face. Silence.*

A: Can I get you another?

D: Why not, I'm not driving.

> *A exits.*

I've been trying to call you. Your number's disconnected.

C: They tend to do that when you don't pay your bill.

D: You could've called me.

C: I don't call people when I'm working.

D: Right. Your delicate process.

> *C stands and approaches her.*

C: I missed you.

She studies his eyes. A returns and hands D a glass of wine.

D: Why are all actors such terrible liars.

Beat.

Production said you're not staying at the motel.

C: No. I'm staying here.

D: I see that.

C: In the spare room.

D: Why.

C: *It just sits there.*

Beat.

I was invited. That okay with you.

Silence.

A: The three of us are old friends. We've been catching up.

D: The three of you.

A: Yes, my wife. She's in the film too.

Silence.

Of course … we'd love to have you stay here as well.

Beat.

D: And you say he didn't mention me.

C: If you can't say something nice.

Beat.

It didn't come up.

D: Thought I told you to get that looked at.

A: Are you always this mean to each other.

D: Only in public.

C: When we're alone we throw knives.

D: Blindfolded.

C and D stare at each other.

A: I'm gonna go stand in the kitchen, anyone want anything?

C: A suit of armour?

D: How 'bout an alibi.

A: (*exiting*) 'We were at the movies, Officer, *His Girl Friday*.'

C: Traitor. Good choice, though.

They stare at each other. Silence.

It's good to see you.

Beat.

You look great.

Beat.

I'm sorry.

He kisses her.

D: How long have we been together.

Beat.

C: I have to get some air.

> *He starts to exit. A pack of matches falls out of his pocket.*

D: You dropped your matches.

> *He stops, turns around, looks at them. She picks them up and holds them out.*

Your matches. You dropped them.

B: How long have you been together.

> *SHIFT.*

D: (*still staring at him*) In human years?

> *He takes the matches from her and exits.*

On and off since the beginning of time.

B: On and off?

D: Well, more like around and around, actually. If you take a piece of film and feed it through a projector, then twist the ends and splice them together, it makes a Möbius strip. A continuous surface with only one side. That twisted little figure eight will run for a thousand years if you let it. One endless reel, the same set of actions playing out over and over again – left to right, right to left, the truth and its reflection. Forever and ever until the end of the world.

B: 'The end of the world.'

D: Film's answer to Purgatory.

B: Why don't you just stop the projector.

D: What kind of self-respecting masochist would do that.

B: Do you love him.

> *Beat.*

Sorry. I don't know why I asked that.

D: No, that's okay. Depends on which side of the film strip we're on.

B: I thought there was only one side.

D: Clever girl.

B: Does he love *you?*

> *Beat.*

D: I'm not sure his brain works like that.

B: His brain?

D: Yeah, his brain. Where do you think it comes from, love fairies? The heart's a muscle, you do know that, right. It's a pump for moving blood around the body. It's not *actually* a factory that stores and manufactures love.

B: So you're a romantic then.

D: Scientists just discovered the chemical in the brain that causes the feeling of being in love. Turns out: the brain can only make it for the first six months of a relationship. The rest is just a memory. Like seeing the face of someone who died in your mind.

B: What's the difference. If it's real in your mind then it's real, isn't it?

D: The difference. Is time. The further away the memory gets, the harder it is to hold on to. Until one day you just remember that you used to remember.

B: That's the worst thing I've ever heard.

D: I read it in a magazine.

B: *Stop buying that magazine.*

D: Not knowing something doesn't stop it from being true.

B: So, according to you, love is just a dead memory.

D: Not me. Science.

B: And what are we supposed to do with this information.

D: How about another drink.

> *She drains her glass.*

You sure you won't join me. I don't like to drink alone. I'll do it, but I don't like it.

> *B gets the wine out of the fridge and pours a glass for each of them.*

You keep your red wine in the fridge?

B: They say you can do whatever you want now.

D: And this is what you want?

B: I don't know. I just sort of do it.

> *Beat.*

D: How long have you two been together.

B: Since school. Back when he thought he was an actor.

D: We're all actors.

> *B raises her glass.*

B: 'All the world's a soundstage,
And all the men and women merely day players.'

> *D raises hers.*

D: 'And one man in his time breaks many hearts.'

> *They drink.*

Are you in love with him.

B: Who.

D: Your *husband*.

> *Beat.*

B: Yes.

D: Is *he* in love with *you*.

> *Beat.*

B: Yes.

D: Sounds great.

B: It is.

D: You've convinced me.

B: What is *wrong with you?*

D: I'm chasing a memory around a Möbius strip, what's your excuse.

B: I don't feel good …

D: Have you slept with him yet.

> *Beat.*

B: Only on camera.

Beat.

D: Might want to keep your eye on that. His fiction has a way of bleeding into his fact.

B: Well, mine doesn't.

D: You sure about that.

Beat.

It's funny. The first time we fall in love. The first time it ends. How do we all know how to behave in those situations. Because we've seen them a million times. They've been shot through our eyes and tattooed onto our brains since birth. We've been raised on replicas. So we learn to become them.

Beat.

What's wrong. You don't look well.

B: (*moving to the floor*) I think I need to lie down …

D: Head rush?

B: Heart attack.

D: (*exiting*) Hang on, I think I have some heroin in my purse …

B crawls to the couch and pulls herself up onto it.

B: I feel like I'm dying.

SHIFT.

The shadow of a ceiling fan casts her in alternating light and dark.

Like I'm being crushed, like … there's this giant bird, perched on my chest, digging its claws into me, like … something terrible's going to happen. Something no one can predict. Like we thought the world was this endless field stretching out in front of us, when really we're on the edge of this cliff we've all got our backs to. We think we're safe, but one step backward and … Or maybe we're already falling. Maybe that's what this feeling in my chest is. We're falling. We just won't find out until we hit the bottom. And then it won't matter. I walk around all day listening to my heart in my ears and I just want to scream, 'Can't you *hear* that? Can't you feel what's *happening* to us?'

Silence.

I know what you're going to say: I shouldn't speak for everyone, I should just speak for me.

I feel like breaking something. I feel like hurting something. Okay, here's one:

It's night. And I'm chasing this man down the side of a highway. All these people in their cars driving past, all safe and warm, flying past us, not knowing we're out there, that this terrible thing is about to happen just a few feet away. He runs down into this deep ditch and I chase after him. And then I look down, and I see that I'm holding a gun. I can hear him pleading with me as he runs.

Then I shoot him in the back and he sort of falls forward and his jacket kind of flutters out around him so that I can't really see him. He's not even dead yet and the world's already swallowing him. I look down and watch him try to breathe. Watch his jacket going up and down …

I empty the rest of the gun into him and it sounds like … dry twigs snapping. Like nothing. And then his jacket stops moving. And I can't see him at all.

I walk back up to the highway and there's this bus there now, parked on the shoulder. It's one of those dream things, like, 'Why is there a bus there.' But there is. And there's all these people inside, lit up with those little overhead lights. I can see them, but they can't see me. Anyway, as the bus pulls away I lob the gun up onto the roof. And then I smile. Because I know that they'll never find me.

Then I turn around and walk into the dark.

It's funny, I never see his face.

I guess if I did, it would be me, right. That's how it works. The man is me. The people in the bus are me, the cars …

My husband says he doesn't have dreams, but he talks in his sleep. I don't know if he doesn't remember or if he just doesn't want to tell me. I used to think being with a writer, your life would be so full of words and stories, but of course it isn't. It's very quiet. It's like he doesn't want to waste it on me, doesn't want to use it up. He never talks to me. Sometimes I wonder why he puts me in his films. Sometimes I wish he wouldn't. People talk. It's embarrassing.

(laughing) It's funny, I really have no idea how I got here. No idea at all.

When I was young I was a lifeguard at a pool, I was a really strong swimmer. I used to like holding my breath underwater. I could stay down a long time. It felt like hours. When I'd come back up, it didn't even feel like I had to, it was more like … I just got tired of holding my breath. The other lifeguards used to get mad. The first time I did it one of them actually dove down and tried to rescue me. He thought I was drowning. It must have been strange, diving down to save someone's life and then getting shoved away. I wonder what he said when he came back up. 'The drowning girl just wants to be left alone.'

I think I'm done. I don't want to come here anymore. I'm tired of just talking about things.

Okay. Here's one more. For the road:

I'm at the bottom of this lake. And I'm running out of air. And it's freezing, colder than anything I've ever felt, but I don't go numb. I can feel all of it, every last bit. It feels like I'm dying. And then I remember: all I have to do is swim back up to the top. The water's thick from the cold, it's like I have to push it behind me, kick it away from me, and I'm wearing this ridiculous red dress that feels like it weighs a thousand pounds – I keep getting tangled up in the material. But finally I get to the surface … And it's frozen. I can't break through. I'm going to drown after all. I can feel my lungs about to explode … And then he's there. Under the water with me … And he smiles at me … He reaches out his hand and I take it, and it's so warm, it's not cold at all, and I figure, 'Hell, if he can do it, so can I.' So I open my mouth … and breathe. But it's just freezing water, it pours itself into me. I'm drowning from the inside out. And I'm so tired, I just want to fall away into the dark, but he won't let go of my hand. He starts squeezing it tighter. I can feel all the little bones start to break, they sound like dry twigs. And he still won't let go of my hand. He just keeps looking at me and smiling …

That wasn't a dream. It was an accident during a film shoot, a short my husband wrote while we were in school, before we were married. He had to jump in and rescue me.

We shot on that lake all day. The paramedics said I had hypothermia. They said I almost died.

What can you do.

D: What can I do.

SHIFT.

A: You grab the glasses, I'll pour the appetizers.

The other three enter and 'set the table.' A leans down and kisses B's forehead.

You sure you're all right.

She stays on the couch as they orbit around her.

B: I'm just tired, that's all. I think these last-minute rewrites are starting to catch up with me.

C: Yeah, are you almost done with those? Today felt like a bit of an ambush.

A: Sorry about that. I just can't seem to make the words sit still.

B: It makes it kind of hard to prepare when your lines keep changing.

D: Isn't that the actor's nightmare.

C: I always get the one where it's opening night and we forgot to rehearse.

B: Oh god, I get that.

C: What's the writer's nightmare.

A & D: Actors.

A: That, or a blank page with the number one in the corner.

B: (*to D*) What about you. What's your anxiety dream.

D: One endless take with no options, no coverage.

   Beat.

B: But … isn't that just … life?

   Beat.

D: Huh. I suppose it is. Maybe that's why we dream; our brains need something to cut away to so we don't go crazy.

A: It's funny, I can't remember my dreams anymore. I wonder when that started …

B: Ever get that thing where everything goes photo-negative?

D: Nope.

A: Can't say that I have.

C: I'm gonna say yes so you don't feel like you're going crazy, but no.

D: (*approaching C*) That's good of you.

C: Well, I'm a really good person.

D: Are you.

> *C and D kiss.*

B: Seriously, no one's ever had that before?

A: I'm sure it's nothing.

D: You're probably just dying.

> *The three of them laugh.*

B: I'm surrounded by jackals.

A: Jackals feeding on sirloin strip.

B: Didn't we have steak last night.

D: Life is suffering.

C: I wonder what the poor people are doing.

A: Watching movies, hopefully.

B: I don't feel good …

C: Well, you look great.

> *He sees D looking at him.*

We all look great.

A: It's the lighting. I paid a lot of money for us to look this good. You'll also notice that all the mirrors in the house are the good kind that make you look cool, not the bad kind that show all your flaws.

B: What? What are you talking about, two kinds of mirrors.

A: Nothing, some mirrors lie and some mirrors tell the truth, that's all. Now if you'd all care to crawl to the table, the first course is served.

They move to the table, a single glass of wine at each place setting.

B: Two kinds of mirrors … I wonder which image other people see.

D: In my experience, the ugly one.

C: Maybe it depends on who's looking at you.

A: Yes. That must be it. Speaking of which:

He raises his glass to B.

Here's lookin' at you, kid.

C and D raise their glasses and drink. B does not.

(*to B*) What's wrong. Not thirsty.

Beat.

B: I'm just not feeling well …

A: Maybe it was something you ate.

Silence.

I had this idea once, for a book – or maybe it's a movie, yeah, make it a movie, we can pay off the house, there you go, decision made: movie – where, and I mean there's a lot of things going on, but one of the secondary or maybe even tertiary plots is that there are these two people who are having an affair telepathically.

I forget where the idea came from. A foreign film, maybe.

Anyway, I had this idea where, you know, what if you were married. Or had a partner. That you loved. That you thought you loved – you felt that you loved this person. And they loved you. Or they thought or felt that they did. And you thought or felt that they did. And you were happy. And then one day the woman discovers, quite accidentally, that she has this psychic link with another man.

They can talk to each other without talking, without even being in the same room. At first, they're not even sure it's really happening. And it's never a main point of focus, the novel's just a – or movie, rather, moviemoviemovie! – the movie's just a, you know, series of 'things that happen.' Events, conflicts, complications, plot points – A, B, C, D and so forth. Two of the characters just happen to be able to speak to each other telepathically. And, you know, she's never, this is not something that she *does*. Neither of them have ever experienced anything like this with anyone else, but … nonetheless. There it is: this link. Now: as her partner. How do you deny that. I mean of course you don't know about it, but even if you did. How could you deny it. A connection like that. And how can *she* deny it. You know, maybe she doesn't even particularly like this guy. Maybe it's not even about eyes-across-a-crowded-room and chemistry and pheromones, but still, the fact remains: *they can sit inside each other's hearts*. And speak without speaking. And so each feel perfectly how the other feels.

How can that be denied. As anything but the truest of love.

Silence.

And as I said, it's a very tertiary plot point, it's not the focus. I think I got the idea from a foreign film: this gypsy boy can move things with his mind but never does anything useful with it. Do you know the one I mean.

C: No.

A: (*to B*) *You've* seen it.

B: I don't think so.

A: No, I'm saying: you've seen it. I know you have, I showed it to you. You've seen it.

B: Oh.

> *Beat.*

Okay. Ask me again.

> *Beat.*

A: Anyway, that's what this would be like. This remarkable thing that never comes into play.

D: In the *play?* I thought you said it was a movie.

A: What? No, into play, into play. I'm not writing a play, Jesus, why don't I just write a poem in Sanskrit. No, I'm saying, it never comes into play, it never gets dealt with. The reader might not even – not reader, audience. Oh god, maybe it is a book. No. It's a movie, dammit, it's ninety pages and I'm selling it for a million dollars. Stars will play them and it will be terrible.

C: What's the point.

A: I beg your pardon?

C: If they don't do anything about it. What's the point.

Beat.

A: The point. Is love.

Beat. B explodes into laughter. Eventually it subsides. Silence. They drink. A drains his glass.

Anyway, my idea was: in the end, (*to C*) it turns out the guy's a liar. *She's* never experienced it before, but *he* can do it with anyone, and he can turn it on and off like a faucet. And when he gets bored with her that's exactly what he does. He's not her true love after all. He's just some asshole who can get inside people's heads.

Beat.

It's just an idea I had.

Beat.

C: I like it. When do we shoot.

A: Whenever you're ready, partner.

Silence. Offstage, a smoke alarm begins to beep. Smoke begins to billow in from the kitchen.

B: (*standing*) Oh, shit. (*exiting*) I thought you turned it off.

A: (*following after*) I did.

D and C remain seated.

B: (*off*) Well obviously you *didn't*, did you! Stop waving at it, it's not a *taxi*!

A: (*off*) You know what, why don't you yell at me more, maybe *that* would help!

B: (*off*) Just get on a stool and take it down!

A: (*off*) You're a real treat, you know that!

>   *The sound of a scraping stool and A climbing up on it.*

A: (*off, a sharp yelp*) AGH!

>   *The sound of the smoke alarm clattering to the floor and stopping.*

(*off*) GODDAMN IT!

>   *Beat. The oven timer begins to buzz.*

(*calling from off*) Dinner's ready.

B: (*off*) At least we know it's *dead* this time.

>   *D drags the table away from C and exits.*

C: I'm sorry.

>   *SHIFT.*

>   *C sits alone, trapped in a harsh down-pool of light. The buzzer fades away. He takes a moment.*

Forgive me.
Forgive me, for I have sinned.
This is my first and last confession.

>   *Silence.*

I have had impure thoughts.
I have been irresponsible.
I have been young and stupid.
I have been old and set in my ways.
I have not accepted God into my heart. Which … makes this whole thing a bit problematic.

I have taken God's name in vain, both casually and with complete conviction.

I have had gods before God, and grown up trying to emulate them.

I have made of myself an idol, to be worshipped.

I have made a willow cabin at your gate.

I have been lustful. Gluttonous. Greedy. Lazy. Vengeful. Jealous. And proud.

I have committed adultery. Almost to memory.

I have coveted my neighbour's wife. Repeatedly.

I have stolen, and called it mine.

I have lied, and made a decent living at it.

I have killed, and been praised for it.

I have eaten red meat on Friday, and enjoyed it.

I have worked on Sunday, and received overtime for it.

I have dishonoured my mother and father, and rarely visit or send cards.

I have been restless.

I have wandered.

I have been a good thief.

I have been the bad son.

I have eaten from the bad apple, and so become one.

I have murdered my brother.

I have hated.

I have loved.

I have lied about loving.

I have hated the one that I loved.

I have received love and not given it.

I have given love and not received it.

I have made love while thinking of another.

I have said 'I love you' while thinking of another.

I have had doubts.

I have been distracted.
I have been thoughtless.
I have been selfish.
I have thought mainly about myself.
I have wished harm.
I have inflicted harm.
I have tried to be happy.
I have done this.
I have done all of this.
And I am not sorry.
Please.
Help me.
Please.
I'm so scared.
Please.
I want love.
I want only love.

> *Silence.*

Are you there?
Is anyone there?

> *Silence. He breaks out of it, looks out.*

Thanks.

> *He gets up and clears the chair, grabs his bag and puts on his jacket.*

Sorry, I kinda got lost there for a minute.

> *Beat.*

I've been away from theatre for a while, but ... I'd love to come back.

He starts to exit, then stops.

Listen … I know I'm not right for this, but … Thank you for seeing me.

He tries to exit … but A is there, waiting for him.

A: That's it? No big speeches. No fond farewells.

SHIFT.

You were just gonna sneak off into the night again?

C: Speeches are really more your thing.

Silence.

A: I've been working on this new one that ends with me punching you in the stomach. Knocking the wind out of you. Dropping you to the floor. Standing over you, watching you fight to breathe …

Silence.

But … in the end … that's not really me, is it.

C: Not really. I've always envied your restraint.

A: Is that what it was.

Beat.

It never goes the way you want, does it. That's the trouble with real life, it's got no sense of resolution. Although it does seem to have a pretty good feel for irony.

Beat.

Fuck you. What do you know about what is and isn't me.

C: Nothing. Not one thing.

A: You were my friend.

C: I remember.

A: What happened.

C: I guess we grew up.

A: No. *I* grew up. You stayed a child.

> *Beat.*

You were my friend. I would've done anything for you.

> *Silence.*

C: You want to know what you did?

> *Beat.*

You want to know what you did for me?

> *Silence. C tries to leave.*

A: Do you love her.

> *Silence.*

How long.

> *Beat.*

How long have you –

C: Since forever. Since the day you brought her through the door.

> *Silence.*

A: The whole time?

Beat.

You were fucking the whole time?

C: No. I was in love with her the whole time. We only fucked when you wrote it into the script.

Silence.

You did this.

D: Who did this?

SHIFT.

C exits. A drops into a chair, his back to us. B stands apart from them, lost in her own world.

A: I got mugged.

He lifts his face to D.

D: *Jesus …*

D dials the telephone, then runs a washcloth under the kitchen tap, cradling the phone in her neck.

A: What are you doing.

D: What do you think I'm doing, I'm calling the police.

D dabs at his eye with the washcloth.

A: (*sucking air*) Don't do that.

D: (*handing him the washcloth*) Fine, you do it.

A: (*taking it*) No, I mean don't call the police.

D: You're in shock, you're not thinking.

B: Hang up the phone.

A: I'm always thinking, it's my tragic flaw.

D: You're not making any sense.

A: Would you hang up the goddamn –
     Jesus, what's taking so long, are you on hold?

D: It's ringing.

A: It's *ringing*? I could be dead by now. When they answer tell
     them you want to talk to a manager.

D: I don't think they have managers.

A: Everyone has managers.

     D notices B just standing there.

D: Hey. You awake? You want to help me out here?

B: What should I do.

D: I don't know. Use your imagination. Find something to take
     down the swelling.

     *As A and D continue, B methodically walks to the fridge, removes
     a raw steak on a plate and unwraps it.*

D: Who did this?

A: I dunno, buncha visible minorities. And I know what you're
     gonna say but they were.

D: What'd they look like?

A: Brown eyes, average height, medium build. Just a matter of
     time 'til they bring 'em in.

D: They didn't take your watch?

A: Must've been a political thing.

D: Where did this happen?

A: The face and ribs, mostly.

D: Stop talking in punchlines!

A: Stop giving me setups.

> *Beat.*

D: Why didn't they take your watch.

> *Silence. D watches B methodically walk forward and offer the steak to A.*

B: Here.

> *A stares at the steak B holds out to him, then looks up at her.*

Always works in the movies.

> *He continues to stare up at her.*

A: You're so beautiful …

> *Beat.*

How do I forget how beautiful you are?

> *D stares at them, B still holding the steak out to A.*

B: Take it.

> *He does. A and B continue to stare at each other.*

D: What is this.

B: Hang up the phone.

Beat. She does. Silence.

D: Where is he.

Beat.

What's going on.

C: Hey, what's goin' on.

SHIFT.

C is sitting on the bed.

You gonna come in or you just gonna stand there.

Beat.

It's not exactly the Park Hyatt, but at least / we can –

D: Do you love me.

Silence.

C: What are you / talking about.

D: *Do you love me.*

Silence.

It's a simple yes or no question.

C: No.

Beat.

It isn't.

Beat.

I … Yes. Sometimes. I'm sorry but that's the truth. Sometimes … Sometimes I really feel like I do.

D: And then other times …

   Beat.

C: I don't know.

D: You don't know. I don't understand that.

C: Neither do I.

D: Either you do or you don't.

C: It's complicated.

D: Explain it to me.

C: I can't.

D: What am I supposed to do with that.

C: I don't know.

D: You don't–?
   Do you know *anything?*

C: I don't know.

D: What is *wrong* with you?

C: I don't know!

D: Stop yelling at me!

C: I'm not yelling at you, I'm yelling at me! Do you think this is fun
   for me? Do you think I like this?

D: I think you thrive / on this!

C: Stop yelling at me!

D: I haven't even *started* yelling at you! And frankly, at this point,
   I will do anything I damn well please.

C: All right.

D: You don't get a say anymore. Your vote is no longer valid.

C: You're right, go / ahead.

D: Don't tell me I'm right, don't say 'go ahead,' like you're giving me permission, like I'm your goddamn / child.

C: Okay.

D: Don't say okay, it is not okay.

C: Okay – Sorry – I won't. I won't say anything.

D: I am so tired of this. The same thing, over and over / again.

C: This isn't the same.

D: How is this any different.

> *Silence.*

Do you love her.

> *Beat.*

C: Yes.

> *Beat.*

D: Guess that question was less complicated.

C: I just, I want to tell you the truth.

> *She explodes into laughter.*

D: What a fantastic time for you to start doing that, when it's most helpful to us. You should really start doing more comedy, your timing is *immaculate*. Where has this wonderful honesty been hiding the whole time we've been together, while you wasted years of my life. This is my life, do you understand that? Do you? *Do you understand that you have fucked up my life.*

C: It was my life, too.

D: No. It's still yours. You made this decision. You made this decision for / both of us.

C: I didn't decide, it just *happened*.

D: Don't do that, don't compare yourself to me in this, you are *nothing* like me. Because I have had no say. *It's not fair.* Why do you get to do this? Why is it up to you?

C: It shouldn't be, I'm sorry.

D: Don't do that, don't say you're sorry. You've done this, you don't get to be sorry too. My heart is gone. *I feel like my heart is gone.*

> *Beat.*

I can't even look at you. You don't even look like you anymore.

> *Silence.*

> *Say something.*

C: … I feel like I'm boxing with broken arms.

D: Don't quote dialogue at me, I've seen the rushes.

C: I don't know what to say. I can't feel anything. Nothing feels real. Just … tell me what to do. I need you to tell me what to do. Tell me what to do, okay, and I'll do it. Just tell me what to do.

> *Beat.*

D: Does she love you.

> *Silence.*

C: I don't know.

    Beat.

D: You really don't know anything at all, do you. Unbelievable. You've torn my life apart and you don't even *know anything*.

    She moves to leave, then turns back.

You know what the worst part is? I still have to edit. For the next three months I have to live this over and over again. I have to watch you meet, and flirt, and kiss, and make love on the fucking floor and fall in fucking *love*. And I have to make it look good. I have to make them love you for that. That's my *job*.

C: Don't do it. Walk away.

D: No. It's going to be me. Some of us don't get to walk away. Some of us have to stay and clean up the mess.

    Beat.

You know what I think? I think you're going to regret this really soon. And for the rest of your life. Because I am *amazing*.

    Beat.

And I think we could have made each other really happy. If you hadn't worked so goddamn hard to fuck it all up.

C: You might be right.

D: They say that life is short and that that's a tragedy. Well … I'm here to tell you: you make the wrong choice and sometimes life is very, very long. You go left when you should have gone right … and sometimes life is endless.

    Beat.

I hope you die alone. I don't say that from anger, I really mean it. With my whole body, I swear to god, I hope that for you.

Silence.

You really love her?

Beat.

You might want to tell her that.

Beat.

C: I did.

Silence.

D: I'm sorry I missed that.

Beat.

I would've liked to have heard how that sounded.

Beat.

And what did she say.

Beat.

C: She said goodbye.

Beat.

D: It never goes the way you want, does it.

Silence. She moves to leave.

C: What are you doing.

D: I'm waking up.

C: I love you.

D: I love you too. Goodbye.

A: Hello.

> *SHIFT.*

> *C is gone. A sits alone in the dark, drinking red wine.*

Didn't expect to see you again.

> *Beat.*

Pretty sure dinner's cancelled.

> *Beat.*

D: I just came back for my notes.

A: Sure. If you see anything else you like … feel free.

> *Beat. She crosses, grabs her notes, then moves to exit.*

How's it going.

> *Beat.*

D: How's it *going?*

A: Yeah. The film. How's it cutting together.

> *Beat.*

D: It's cutting fine.

A: Good.

> *Beat.*

D: I'm not sure your ending works.

A: Oh. That's too bad.

Beat.

But besides that? Besides the ending? No other problems?

Silence.

D: There's always problems. Nothing I can't handle.

Beat.

I could have used more coverage. And in my opinion the darks are too dark and the lights are completely blown out. But it's a bit late to do anything about that now. If they can't fix it in the transfer I guess we'll just have to pretend we did it on purpose. Or maybe we did. No one really discussed it with me.

Beat.

The movie's going to be fine. I'll just have to be creative. It'll be fine.

A: Glad to hear it.

Beat.

D: It might even be good. When it's all finished. I'm almost through the last of the rushes. You should sit in sometime.

A: I'll take a rain check.

Beat.

D: At the very least, it would be nice to have a conversation with you at some point, about your intention.

A: My intention?

D: With the script. The reason you wrote it. So that I'm not working at cross-purposes. It would be useful to know what your intention was.

Beat.

A: There wasn't one. I don't write from theme. It's just a story I thought of.

Silence.

D: What was wrong with the first editor.

Beat.

A: I don't know. I guess he wasn't working out. Production fired him.

D: No. They didn't. You did. Before he cut a fucking frame.

Silence.

A: He didn't relate to the material.

Silence.

D: Where is she.

Beat.

A: She's gone.

She moves to exit.

It's funny how everyone thinks they're the main character. The one everyone's been rooting for. Then one day, you wake up and you realize … nobody's been watching you at all. You see the final cut, and you're barely in frame. All your good stuff got left on the floor. All your darlings got murdered. They didn't respond to you in the test screenings. So they decided to go another way.

Beat.

D: How drunk are you.

A: How extended was that metaphor.

> *He wells up.*

I'm lost. I don't know where I am. How did I get here?

D: Hard work and sacrifice.

A: I don't even feel like me. I feel like I'm watching myself, like I'm dreaming. Like I could do anything.

D: Occupational hazard.

> *Beat.*

A: Can I buy you a drink.

D: I'll take a rain check.

> *He kisses her. She pulls away.*

A: What.

D: It's a bit predictable, isn't it?

A: Predictable?

D: I think I've seen this one before. I think I know how it ends.

> *Beat.*

A: No. You don't. No one knows …

> *He kisses her again, gently. They lie down on the couch. He moves down to her neck … her chest … her stomach, pushing up her shirt … then moves up to her mouth again, straddling her. He moves his hands to her face … down to her neck … She starts to choke. He's strangling her, pushing down on her throat with his whole body.*

A terrible, extended moment, until finally …
He lets her go. She coughs, fighting to breathe.

Oh God. Oh Jesus. I'm sorry. I'm sorry …

He flees as she continues to cough, the coughing becoming amplified.

D: … Sorry.

SHIFT.

A lecture hall. Clips of black-and-white film noir love scenes play behind, much like the final scene in Cinema Paradiso.

Something went down the wrong way.

She clears her throat and drinks from a glass of water.

Where am I.

She refers to her notes, then looks behind her, at the film clips.

Right.

Beat.

The temptation … is to leave your mark. Initials under the seat. A flaw in the rug. Something, anything, that says, 'I was here. I existed.'

We must resist that temptation. We are magicians, but our trick is to be invisible. Our calling card must be blank. No one can ever think of us. If they do, something is very, very wrong.

They say a film is born three times: once when it's written, once again when it's shot, and once, finally, when it's edited. Sometimes, the first two births go well, and your birth … is a painless one. It's like a dream. Everything makes sense. The way forward is as simple and perfect as a straight black line. All you have to do is follow it faithfully, to the end. But often, the first two births are *not* easy births. There are complications. Things go wrong. Moments are lost. Mistakes are made. What looked good on the page often is not. What felt great on the day often was not. *We* are left with the pieces. Both the ones we have and the ones we don't, the ones that are missing. All we have is what we are given. We can make nothing, we can create nothing. We can only interpret, suggest associations, by proximity, in the hope that … something might be understood. We are not weavers, we are quilt-makers. We are scavengers, searching through the rubble, sorting through the mess. To use that which appears unusable. To save that which appears unsalvageable. To make sense … of the senseless.

The film clips repeat, this time flipped left to right.

Sometimes this can be difficult. Sometimes, almost impossible. And *sometimes* … it *is* impossible. Sometimes the mess wins. And no one knows why. Everyone tried. Everyone did their best. But, in the end, it's still a mess. It's not your fault. You're just the one left sitting in it. *It is not your fault.* There'll be another one. Sometimes you won't *want* there to be another one … But there will be. And if you're lucky, it'll be better. And if you're *really* lucky … it'll be amazing.

But you know what? Even if it is amazing. It's still a mess. That's what they don't tell you. It's all just a mess, the whole thing. Even on the good days, it's a sort of … nightmare that you have to live inside. That you have to learn. Every foot. Every frame. Until you know it by heart. Until you see it when you close your eyes at night. Until you really do dream it. And then waking up. Trying to make it better. Trying to make it perfect.

And failing.

Endlessly … endlessly failing.

B crosses, dropping a matchbook. C follows after her, picking it up.

The whole thing's a nightmare.

C: You dropped your matches.

    SHIFT.

    B stops, turns around, looks at him.

B: That the best you can do.

    D stares out from behind the podium, reflected light from their moving image playing across her face.

C: Your matches. You dropped them.

B: Thanks.

    She pockets them and withdraws a cigarette.

Got a light.

    He looks at her, confused. Then smiles. He withdraws a Zippo, tries to light it. Nothing. Again. Nothing. Again. Nothing. She tries not to smile. Again. Nothing. He looks out.

C: This lighter doesn't work.

    She explodes into laughter.

My lighter doesn't work.

    He watches her laugh, smiling.

You are so not going home with me. (*out*) Thanks, everybody, great first day, you've officially broken my spirit!

B: (*out*) Okay, where should we go from, where are we.

C: I think we're in hell. Are we still rolling?

B: I think so.

C: Should we maybe cut? I know I'm just a lowly actor but I feel like this footage is maybe not so usable.

B: Deleted scene.

C: My life's a deleted scene. Should we not cut? What's happening. Isn't film stock expensive.

B: We're shooting on film?

C: Figure of speech.

B: (*out, mocking*) I can't work like this, is it too late to recast?

C: (*pretending to call out to someone*) Stunt double!

    They go to black. Beat.

D: Master usable before lighter snap. Note for sound, laugh may be useful elsewhere. Scene 27-B, take 3.

    Lights back up. B crosses but forgets to drop the matches. She immediately crosses back.

B: I guess maybe I should drop my matches.

    C steps in.

C: If you want. You know, only if you're feeling / it.

    She walks past him.

B: Shut / up.

C: (*following her off*) It makes it easier for me to say, 'You dropped your matches,' / but I don't want to make your choices for you.

B: (*off, laughing*) Shut up!

C: (*off*) I can find a new motivation if you're trying / something.

B: (*off, laughing*) Stop being a jerk!

C: (*off*) That's like asking a cat to stop chasing birds.

B: (*off*) Then go chase a bird!

C: (*off*) You know what, I don't think this is gonna work.

> *She laughs. They go to black.*

D: Unusable. Note for production: *why did you print this.* Scene 27-B, take 6.

> *Lights back up. B crosses, drops her matches, C chases after her, picks them up.*

C: You dropped your matches! (*immediately putting them down and exiting*) Can we do that / again.

B: (*picking them up and exiting*) We sure / can.

C: (*off*) I was like a newsie from the twenties.

B: (*off*) We still going? / Okay.

C: (*off*) All right, Take 7: The Revenge of Take 6, go.

> *B enters as before, drops her matches, C chases after, picks them up.*

You dropped your matches.

> *B stops, turns around, looks at him.*

B: That the best you can do.

C: Your matches. You dropped them.

B: Thanks.

She pockets them and withdraws a cigarette.

Got a light.

He looks confused, then smiles. He lights her cigarette with his Zippo. She inhales and exhales luxuriously.

C: Have we met before.

B: *(exiting)* Why don't you quit while you're ahead.

He watches her go. Looks down at his Zippo. Smiles. Another moment, then looks out.

C: And *that* is how you do it downtown!

She re-enters, coughing and holding the cigarette out.

B: These are / disgusting.

C: It's called being a professional, ladies and gentlemen.

D smiles at C's obnoxious charm before remembering herself.

B: Where should I put this out.

C: *(running to her)* No, no, give it to me!

He reaches for the cigarette as they go to black.

D: Best take. Useable after second start. Scene plays in master. Scene 44-A, take 12.

Lights back up. B stands in the foreground, facing out, C stands in the background, talking to her.

C: Let's run away.

B: What, are we orphans.

C: Wayward youths. Babes in the wood. A pair a modern-day Oliver Twists.

B: Have you even *read Oliver Twist.*

C: I skimmed the dirty parts. We're a regular coupla Lost Boys.

B: That's *Peter Pan.*

C: Same difference.

B: And I'm a girl.

C: So I've noticed.

> *He kisses her neck from behind.*

Let's pretend we're alone …

B: We are alone …

C: (*his arms around her*) Good, that'll make it easy …

B: What if he comes back …

C: (*his hands under her shirt*) There's no one here but us …

B: In the house?

C: (*turning her around*) In the world …

> *He kisses her. D watches as they kiss and grope each other.*

B: Everyone thinks they're the main character …

C: Yeah, but in my case it's actually true …

B: Someone has to play the supporting role …

C: Long as it's not me …

B: You're a real team player …

C: I prefer individual sports …

B: Tell me a story …

C: I love you …

D: Stop.

> *Lights go to black. Silence.*

I'll come back to this.

> *Beat.*

Scene 121-b, take 1.

> *Lights up on B and C, facing each other, not making eye contact, uncomfortable. After a moment, C looks out at someone.*

C: Are we ready?

> *Beat.*

Okay.

> *We see them adjust to begin the scene. She turns away from him. He grabs her arm, spins her back. He grabs her face. Silence.*

C: I love you.

> *Silence.*

B: (*grabbing his face*) I love you too.

> *They kiss.*

Goodbye.

> *She exits. Lights go to black. Silence.*

D: Scene 121-b, take 2, pickup.

Lights up on B and C – C already holding her face. They're look-ing out, still looking uncomfortable with each other.

C: Okay, so you just want us to do a bunch of them in a row and – ? *(listening)* Okay … *(listening)* Right. *(to her)* Ready?

B: Yeah. *(out)* And should I break away every time or – ? *(listening)* Okay. And what's the frame, like here?

She indicates head and shoulders with her hands.

(listening) Okay. So I'll just – *(listening)* Yeah, exactly, okay, no, that's great. *(to him)* Okay, sorry.

C: It's okay. You ready?

B: Yeah.

C: Okay.

Silence.

I love you.

Beat.

B: I love you too.

They kiss.

Goodbye.

She steps out of frame.

B: *(out)* Am I out there? *(listening)* Okay.

She steps back and he takes hold of her again.

C: Is that okay?

B: Yeah.

C: Okay. Again?

B: Yeah.

>*Silence.*

C: I love you.

>*Beat.*

B: I love you too.

>*They kiss.*

Goodbye.

>*She steps out of frame and back. Beat.*

C: I love you.

>*Beat.*

B: I love you too.

>*They kiss.*

Goodbye.

>*She steps out of frame and back. Beat.*

C: I love you.

>*Beat.*

B: I love you too.

>*They kiss.*

Goodbye.

She steps out of frame and back. Beat.

C: I love you.

> *Beat.*

B: I love you too.

> *They kiss.*

Goodbye.

> *She steps out of frame and back. Beat.*

C: I love you.

> *Beat.*

B: I love you too.

> *They kiss.*

Goodbye.

> *She steps out of frame and back. Beat.*

C: I love you.

> *Beat.*

B: I love you too.

> *They kiss.*

Goodbye.

> *She steps out of frame and back. Beat.*

C: I love you.

> *Beat.*

B: I love you too.

> *They kiss.*

Goodbye.

> *She steps out of frame and back. Beat.*

C: I love you.

> *Beat.*

B: I love you too.

> *They kiss.*

Goodbye.

> *She steps out of frame and back. Although they continue to speak, the sound of them is slowly overwhelmed by the final movement of a requiem.*

> *Lights fade on D as she watches them kiss and say I love you and goodbye to each other over and over again …*

> *Black.*

> *Title card: THE END*

End.

A Quiet Place

a comic tragedy in one act

for my father

A Quiet Place was produced by Single Threat, premiering at the Robert Gill Theatre as part of the 2005 Toronto Fringe Festival on July 8, 2005, with the following cast and crew:

Henry: James Cade
David: Christopher Stanton

Direction: Geoffrey Pounsett
Sound Design: Christopher Stanton
Set & Costume Design: Michelle Bailey
Violence: Mark Huisman
Assistant Direction: Melissa Moore
Stage Management: Amy Levett

It was remounted by Single Threat as part of the inaugural Next Stage Festival at the Factory Studio Theatre in January of 2008 with the following cast and crew:

Henry: James Cade
David: Christopher Stanton

Direction & Set Design: Geoffrey Pounsett
Sound Design: Christopher Stanton
Violence: Mark Huisman
Dances: Emily Andrews
Stage Management: Sherry Roher

A Quiet Place was nominated for five 2008 Dora Mavor Moore Awards: Best New Play, Outstanding Production, Outstanding Direction, Outstanding Performance (Christopher Stanton) and Outstanding Sound Design.

Playwright's Note

All scenes take place in a dark room with no door.

The tortoise story is taken and adapted from Charles L. Mee's short play Chiang Kai Chek *with permission from the author (www.charlesmee.org). Additionally, the playwright would like to thank Michel Basilières, Daniel Brooks, Chad Donella, David Ferry, Keira Loughran, Joan MacLeod and Geoffrey Pounsett for reading and responding to various drafts; actors Ben Clost, David Ferry, David Storch and Rylan Wilkie for lending their voices to Henry and David at various points; Melissa Moore and Jane Spence at the Toronto Cold Read Series; Tim Gentle at Pressure of Time; Malcolm Gilderdale for letting me use his apartment in Montreal where I wrote a good deal of the first draft; and Alana Wilcox at Coach House Books for publishing A Quiet Place together with Wide Awake Hearts in book form, even though they were written almost ten years apart. With sincere apologies to anyone he has managed to forget.*

A Quiet Place

Prologue

A voice in the darkness:

HENRY: I love it here. It's so quiet. Sometimes I think this is my
favourite place.

Henry

*Lights up slowly on a small, square room, lit by a single hanging light
bulb. HENRY is doing pushups, his head to us. He continues to the
point of collapse. He rolls onto his back, panting. Once recovered he
gets into the lotus position with his back to us. He breathes. Lights
fade slowly to black.*

The Chair

*Lights up. HENRY observes a red chair now in the centre of the
room. Blackout.*

David

*Lights up slowly as DAVID, unconscious and tied to the chair, comes
to. Henry is sitting in the lotus position facing him, his back to the
audience.*

DAVID: Hey … Hey. What is this? Hey. Hey. Help. Help.

Henry gets up and walks to David.

Someone help me. Anyone.
Oh Jesus help me please.

Henry hits David as hard as he can in the face.

Help. Help.

Henry hits him again, harder. David blacks out with the lights.

Lights up slowly as David comes to. Henry is in the lotus position as before.

Hey. What is this? Why are you doing this?

Henry gets up and walks to David.

No please wait a second please just wait –

Henry hits David as hard as he can in the face. David blacks out with the lights.

Lights up slowly as David comes to. Henry is in the lotus position. Everything is as it was.

DAVID: Hey.

Henry gets up. David shuts his mouth. Henry walks to David and stands, waiting for him to speak. David does not.

HENRY: Good.

Henry grabs David's face and prepares to hit him. David tenses but says nothing. Henry releases David's face.

Good.

Henry walks away.

You were asleep for a long time.

The first time, I mean. Before you woke up the first time.

You sleep like a child, did you know that? Sometimes your eyes move under your eyelids. And sometimes you part your lips. As if you were speaking with someone.

Were you dreaming? Who were you talking to? Or maybe you were alone. Talking to yourself. Were you? It doesn't matter.

I don't have dreams. I'm not even sure I sleep. Does that sound strange? You don't have to answer that.

I've decided you have a very nice face, in an ordinary sort of way. A nice face. A peaceful face.

But you're not ordinary, are you? No. Far from it. Well. Neither am I.

Somos pocos, pero estamos locos.

We extraordinary types need to stick together. Do you speak Spanish? I don't really. I guess it's just one of those phrases you pick up. I'm not crazy. I can tell that you think I am. I'm not.

What's your name?

The quiet game's over now. I'm changing the rules.

What's your name?

I feel like hitting you again. But I'm not going to. I want you to know that. I'm going to try my best to be civilized. I'd like you to do the same.

Henry waits.

DAVID: David. My name is David.

HENRY: David. David. You don't look like a David.

DAVID: I'm sorry.

HENRY: Don't apologize. It's not your fault, is it?

DAVID: No.

HENRY: Exactly. You just don't look like a David, that's all.

DAVID: Did you drug me?

HENRY: Do you feel drugged?

DAVID: Yes.

HENRY: Well, there's your answer, I guess. I expect the feeling will pass. I've also been hitting you a lot. Maybe I should switch to the stomach.

DAVID: Can I say something? I don't think I'm whoever you think I am.

HENRY: Who do I think you are?

DAVID: I don't know. But I don't think I'm him.

HENRY: Who are you?

DAVID: I don't know.

HENRY: What?

DAVID: I just … I can't imagine what you would want with me.

HENRY: You're being awfully hard on yourself. I'm sure you have lots of great qualities. You take a punch better than anyone I've ever met.

DAVID: What do you want? What's your name? What should I call you?

HENRY: You can call me Henry. If you like.

DAVID: But that isn't your name. Why are you doing this, Henry?

Henry closes his eyes.

Or is this your idea? Am I talking to the brains or just the help?

Henry hits David in the stomach, knocking the wind out of him. Henry nurses his hand as he talks.

HENRY: I'm sorry. I know I said you could talk. You can ask questions. I won't stop you. For some reason I thought that would hurt less. What's the matter, David? You seem quiet.

Blackout.

The Experiment

Lights up. Henry is behind David, watching him quietly try to wriggle out of his ropes.

HENRY: Any luck?

David jumps with a start and then freezes.

Please. Continue. Don't give up now, David.

DAVID: I thought you were gone.

HENRY: I think your left thumb is almost free.

Silence. David starts to struggle again. Henry watches.

Hm ... That thumb comment may have been misleading. Must be difficult not being able to see what you're doing. It's like a puzzle, isn't it?

David gives up.

This must be frustrating. If you were a wild animal, a wolf let's say, I bet you could do it. Gnaw through the ropes, your own leg if necessary. Tear out my throat, tear at the walls until your paws were ... You see what I'm saying.

DAVID: I think we should test your theory. Next time you find a wolf, tie him to a chair and see what happens.

HENRY: They say when a scorpion is cornered, rather than let itself be killed, it will sting itself to death. They also say this of a scorpion circled in flame. Sort of childish, if you think about it.

DAVID: I don't believe you.

HENRY: Well. Regardless. I don't think it's really your style. So what's left?

DAVID: Leave me alone.

HENRY: Good, talking. What else?

DAVID: I don't know.

HENRY: Don't be rash, take your time, think about it.

DAVID: I don't want to talk about this.

HENRY: My God, you're right. Here we are. Sitting around, talking about instinct. We need action. I'm going to have to hit you again.

DAVID: Please don't.

HENRY: I'm sorry, I have to.

DAVID: No. Please. Don't do this.

HENRY: As hard as I can. In the face.

DAVID: You said you wouldn't do this.

HENRY: I said I would try.

DAVID: How does this help you?

HENRY: This isn't for me, it's for science. What does your body tell you to do, David?

Henry pulls his fist back, preparing to hit David.

DAVID: No.

Henry brings his fist down in a wide arc, stopping an inch from David's face. David is frozen in fear, his eyes shut.

HENRY: Paralyzing fear. The David Defence. You look like a turtle, we could call it the Turtle Defence. You can open your eyes now, David.

Henry walks away. Blackout.

Henry's Dream

Lights up. Henry is staring at nothing in particular.

DAVID: When do we eat?

HENRY: Are you hungry?

Pause.

DAVID: No. How long have you been up? Don't you get a break? Someone should take over once in a while.

HENRY: I agree.

DAVID: So why don't they? Listen. You could sleep for a while, if you wanted. You look pretty tired. I'm not going anywhere. And I won't tell anyone if that's what you're worried about.

HENRY: Thank you.

DAVID: You should sleep once in a while. It's not good for you.

HENRY: Are you a doctor, David? Am I going to have to pay you for this examination?

DAVID: Your body needs REM sleep. Deep sleep. If your body doesn't get it, you'll suffer for it.

HENRY: REM sleep.

DAVID: Rapid Eye Movement.

HENRY: Your eyes do that sometimes.

Henry demonstrates.

DAVID: Probably means I'm dreaming. They say that's when most dreams take place.

HENRY: I dream when I'm awake. You go crazy if you don't dream. I just do it with my eyes open. Watch:

I'm in a field. Tall blades of grass. A tree without leaves. There's no wind. I'm bathed in sunlight. I'm watching myself. From a great height. Something terrible is going to happen. I'm floating further away. The Sun. The Sun feels so … clean. I can't see myself anymore, I'm too high up. I can't even see the tree. This field goes on forever. There's no end to it. I've never seen anything so …

I want music. I want to hear music.

Henry hums tunelessly to himself. His voice cracks and he begins to sob.

I can't remember any songs. I'm sorry. I'm so sorry.

DAVID: Henry, where's the door?

Henry regains his composure.

HENRY: It's a secret. Where do you think it is?

David tries to look around.

DAVID: Behind me? It must be behind me. Is it?

HENRY: What would you do if you were free?

DAVID: I'd kill you.

HENRY: Don't rush. Take all the time you need.

DAVID: I'd strangle you. Dig my thumbs into your throat. Push until I felt my own fingers through the other side. Right through your neck. I'd watch you die.

HENRY: You've been thinking about this. Well. If I was considering it before, I'm definitely not untying you now. What's so funny?

DAVID: You were never considering it. You'll never let me go. I know what happens.

HENRY: You've been kidnapped, tied to a chair and murdered before?

DAVID: I'm not stupid.

HENRY: Well, you're not smart.

DAVID: Why not do it now? Why drag it out?

HENRY: We're just getting started.

DAVID: Well. I'm done.

HENRY: I'm sorry, are you going somewhere?

DAVID: Goodbye, Henry.

HENRY: Goodbye? Goodbye? Look at me, David.

Henry moves into David's sightline.

Look at me.

David stares through him. Henry grabs David's hair and pulls his head back, forcing David to look directly into his eyes.

That's not for you to say.

David does nothing. Henry releases him.

We'll see.

Henry watches David.

Do you think this is a good idea, David? Terrible things happen to people all the time. Things done that cannot be undone. David. You don't want to do this. David.

Blackout.

Lights up. David stares out vacantly from his chair. Henry is performing what appears to be an eccentric version of tai chi. Blackout.

Lights up. David is the same as before. Henry is doing pushups on his fists. He stops and looks over before resuming. Blackout.

Lights up. David is the same as before. Henry paces behind him, then stops, an idea occurring to him. Henry extends his index finger outward and walks slowly toward David. His finger connects with David's temple and begins to slowly tip him over. David betrays no reaction as he and his chair approach 45 degrees ... Blackout.

The Boy and the Tortoise

Lights up. David is lying on his side, still tied to the chair, still staring out vacantly. Henry is sitting behind him in the lotus position.

HENRY: Would you like to hear a story that was told to me once?

David does not answer.

There was a man who had a son.

And the son had a tortoise.

One day, the father decided, quite without malice, to teach his boy a lesson.

He took the tortoise and placed a burning stick against the shell of its belly.

The heat of the stick caused the shell to crack.

As the tortoise struggled, the father used his knife to slit open its belly and pull out its still-beating heart.

By this time the tortoise had withdrawn into its shell, trying to hide there, its head between its elbows, looking out.

By this time the boy came to see what the father had been doing.

When the boy saw the tortoise, he drew his own elbows up beside his head and looked out, just like the tortoise.

The father and the son watched the tortoise struggle in silence, until it stopped.

The boy wiped his tears and asked the father why he had done this.

The father turned to him and said: A tortoise, like the world, or a man, is a strong, stubborn thing that can live for a while without its heart.

And the boy …

The boy …

Henry falters.

I can't remember any more.

Henry looks at David.

Please talk to me, David. I can't stand this. I was so alone. And then you came, and I wasn't alone anymore. It was a miracle, I think. I think you being here is a miracle. And now you're gone again. (*weeping*) I don't even know if you're real.

DAVID: (*realizing*) You didn't do this.

Henry starts at the sound of David's voice. He moves toward him.

You touch me again and we're done.

Henry stops.

You didn't do this.

HENRY: I'm here like you.

DAVID: What's your name? Your real name.

David stares out vacantly.

HENRY: Henry. I think it's Henry.

David looks back at him.

DAVID: I'm. Having. Trouble. Remembering things.

HENRY: It gets worse.

DAVID: Who's done this, Henry?

HENRY: I don't know. It's the truth, I swear, I don't know. I don't remember seeing anyone.

DAVID: Then how did you get here?

HENRY: I don't know, I was just here.

DAVID: There must have been a moment before.

HENRY: What was yours?

David thinks about this.

DAVID: How long have you been here?

HENRY: A long time.

DAVID: You told me I was your prisoner.

HENRY: I never said that.

DAVID: You let me believe I was your prisoner.

HENRY: I was scared.

DAVID: I'm tied to a chair, Henry.

HENRY: I watched you while you slept. You slept like a child. You moved your lips as though –

DAVID: You hit me.

HENRY: You were asleep for so long. I had too much time to think.

DAVID: Think about what?

HENRY: You were tied to a chair. You were tied down. I just kept thinking: you had to be tied to a chair.

DAVID: So you fucking tortured me?

HENRY: No. No, I never –
I had to scare you, I didn't know –
This is a very small room, David, I had to scare you.

David looks away from Henry and stares out vacantly.

Oh. No. Please talk to me. I'm sorry, David, please. Don't go away again. Don't play the quiet game.

DAVID: I'm not your tortoise.

HENRY: What? I know that. I know that. I know you're not my tortoise. That was just a story. That was just a story I remembered. You're not a tortoise, David.

DAVID: Good. Now untie me.

HENRY: Oh.

DAVID: What.

HENRY: I can't.

DAVID: Of course you can. Of course you can untie me, just –
Just come over here and undo these ropes, Henry. Henry.

HENRY: I can't. I can't. I didn't tie you up.

DAVID: I know that. I believe you.

HENRY: You're meant to be tied up, you had to be tied to a chair.

DAVID: Untie me, Henry. Now.

HENRY: I can't. I'm sorry, David.

David looks away and stares out vacantly.

HENRY: David? David, please. I can't. Don't do this. Why are you doing this?

That's it, then? 'Untie me, Henry, now,' is going to be the last thing you said.

You know this affects me too. This affects me. We don't know what might happen. Every decision we make has –

Everything we do can change … everything. I don't want to make any mistakes.

David continues to stare out vacantly.

All right.

David? I'm going to have to touch you to untie you. Is that all right, David?

I'm taking your silence to mean yes.

Henry approaches David cautiously. He starts to untie him. As soon as he can, David grabs Henry's neck and begins strangling him, bringing him to the floor. Henry struggles but David is stronger. It continues for an unbearable length of time. The lights begin to fade as Henry begins to lose consciousness. At the last possible moment David releases him, the lights surging back, and backs away. Henry gasps and coughs. David picks up the rope and stands over Henry.

DAVID: You were right, Henry. Everything has changed. Where's the door.

HENRY: There isn't one.

Blackout.

Taking the Initiative

Lights up. David is carefully inspecting the walls. Henry is practicing his eccentric version of tai chi.

HENRY: How long are you going to do that for?

DAVID: As long as it takes.

HENRY: You're almost at the part that looks like something but turns out to be nothing.

DAVID: Yeah, what is that?

HENRY: It's nothing.

David watches Henry.

DAVID: How long did you look?

Henry continues his tai chi.

HENRY: I forget.

David continues to watch him.

DAVID: Why do you do that?

HENRY: Do what?

DAVID: What do you think? That. What is that?

HENRY: What do you think it is?

DAVID: I know what you think it is.

HENRY: What do I think it is?

DAVID: You think it's tai chi.

HENRY: It is tai chi. I'd forgotten the word.

DAVID: I –
That is not tai chi, Henry, and in your heart you know it isn't.

HENRY: Sure it is.

DAVID: No. It isn't.

HENRY: Yes. It is.

DAVID: Where'd you learn it? Who taught it to you?

HENRY: I taught myself.

DAVID: You can't teach yourself tai chi.

HENRY: You can't?

DAVID: No.

HENRY: Well then what am I doing?

DAVID: Not tai chi.

HENRY: You're jealous.

DAVID: I am not jealous.

HENRY: Sure you are. You're jealous because I can do tai chi, and you can't.

DAVID: It is physically impossible for someone to teach himself an ancient martial art. It's not like teaching yourself to whistle, Henry.

Henry begins to whistle while he does tai chi.

Fucking tai chi …

HENRY: You swear all the time, did you know that about yourself, David? All the time. Even when you're in a good mood. Even when you're happy.

DAVID: Just admit it, Henry. Admit it's not tai chi.

HENRY: Do you know tai chi, David?

DAVID: No, but that's not –

HENRY: Do you know tai chi?

DAVID: That isn't tai chi, I've been watching you for fucking ever and –

HENRY: (*overlapping*) Just answer the question.

DAVID: (*overlapping*) … you do the same five things over and over –

HENRY: (*overlapping*) Answer the question, David.

DAVID: (*overlapping*) … and over again, and it's driving me fucking crazy.

Henry stops.

HENRY: What are you afraid of? Just answer the question: do you know tai chi?

David stares at him.

DAVID: No.

HENRY: Thank you. Was that so difficult? To admit that you don't know something?
And to answer your question, I do it because it relaxes me.

Henry breathes in sharply and does a ridiculously elaborate and stylized imitation of a crane. Blackout.

Red Light Green Light

Lights up. Henry stands at the upstage wall, facing David who stands downstage, staring out.

DAVID: This room's too small.

HENRY: You're scared.

DAVID: I'm not scared, this room's too small.

HENRY: You're making excuses.

DAVID: It isn't fair.

HENRY: Nothing's fair.

DAVID: No, but this is decidedly –

HENRY: You understood the limitations when you agreed to this.

DAVID: Listen, all I'm saying is Green Light.

Henry bolts forward stretching out his hand to touch David.

Red Light.

Henry freezes, inches from touching him.

HENRY: You are in so much trouble.

DAVID: You think so?

HENRY: Say it.

DAVID: I'm not sure I want to play anymore ...

HENRY: Say, 'Green Light.'

DAVID: I don't feel well ...

HENRY: You're not getting out of this.

DAVID: No ... I'm serious ... I think ... Henry, I think something's happening to me ...

David buckles. Henry moves toward him.

HENRY: David?

DAVID: Ha. You moved, you're out.

HENRY: No. No, I was seeing if you were okay, I –

DAVID: You still moved.

HENRY: That's cheating.

DAVID: No, moving when you're supposed to be frozen is cheating.

HENRY: That's not fair.

DAVID: (*mocking Henry's tai chi*) Nothing is fair.

HENRY: Oh. You are such a –

DAVID: What? What am I?

HENRY: You are … walking the line.

DAVID: The line?

HENRY: What if you were really hurt?

DAVID: What line, we're playing Red Light Green Light.

HENRY: If you were hurt and I did nothing. Because of a game.

DAVID: I guess you'd have to live with that. Every day. Now get up there, it's two–nothing, me.

HENRY: Best three out of five.

DAVID: It's your game.

They take their places, Henry downstage, David up.

HENRY: This room is too small.

DAVID: I'm waiting …

Henry fidgets.

HENRY: Red Light. Red Light. Grrred Light.

Henry looks back. David has not moved. Henry looks forward.

One of these days you're going to make a mistake. And I will be there to watch you fall, and laugh, and laugh, and laugh …

As Henry speaks, David sneaks up behind him, reaching out to touch him. Blackout.

I Spy

Lights up. Henry and David sit against opposite walls. Henry looks around casually.

HENRY: I spy ... with my little eye ... something that is ... red.

David looks at the chair, the only red thing in the room. He sighs. Blackout.

Hide and Seek

DAVID: ... twenty-two, twenty-three, twenty-four, twenty-five ...

Lights up. David stands downstage, his eyes closed. Henry runs around, looking for a hiding spot.

... twenty-six, twenty-seven, twenty-eight, twenty-nine ...

Henry ducks down behind the chair in the corner of the room.

... thirty.

Henry panics and gets up again, looking for somewhere better.

Ready or not, here I come.

Henry changes his mind again and tries to run back behind the chair, but David looks around before he can duck down.

HENRY: Okay. Wait, just –
Okay, sorry –
Can I go again?

David stares at Henry. He turns around and closes his eyes again.

DAVID: One, two, three ...

Blackout.

Tag

Lights up. Henry excitedly attempts to evade David. David pursues Henry unenthusiastically, eventually cornering and tagging him.

Henry tags back. David tags back. Etc., etc. Eventually David gives up completely. He walks away and sits down on the chair.

HENRY: What's wrong?

DAVID: Nothing. I think I need a break.

Henry watches David.

It doesn't make sense. Why can I remember some things and not others? I remember how to speak, but I can't remember anyone I knew. Why can I remember I Spy and not my last name?

Henry looks around.

HENRY: I spy …

DAVID: Henry.

HENRY: Okay.

HENRY: Do you remember any other games?

DAVID: No.

Henry is disappointed. David looks over and notices this.

I remember chess.

HENRY: Oh yeah, chess …

David watches Henry.

DAVID: Do you remember chess?

HENRY: No.

DAVID: You play it on a board.

HENRY: Are you good?

DAVID: I'm all right.

HENRY: You can teach me.

DAVID: Teach you. To play chess. We're missing a few things.

HENRY: Such as?

DAVID: Such as everything you need to play chess. A board. Pieces. A clock, if you want to get fancy.

HENRY: I'd kill for a clock. Well, you can just teach me the rules then. Fundamental chess theory.

DAVID: Maybe.

HENRY: It's something to do. We'll start tomorrow. Good night, David.

> *Henry impulsively hugs David, who tenses visibly. Henry holds the embrace just past the point of comfort before letting go and curling up in a corner. David looks at Henry.*

DAVID: I thought you couldn't sleep.

HENRY: I'm getting better. Since you got here. Good night, David.

DAVID: Night.

> *Henry closes his eyes. David watches him. Blackout.*

Henry's Dream #2

HENRY: Mm ... mm ... mm ...

> *Lights up. David is watching Henry moan in his sleep.*

Oh ... oh ... oh ...

DAVID: Hey. Hey.

HENRY: Mmm?

DAVID: You were talking in your sleep.

HENRY: Was I?

DAVID: Yeah.

HENRY: Sorry about that.

Henry opens his eyes.

What was I saying?

DAVID: You were mumbling.

HENRY: You couldn't make anything out?

DAVID: No.

HENRY: Nothing?

DAVID: I think you might have said, 'Oh.'

HENRY: Oh. Oh. Well … Good night.

Henry closes his eyes again. David watches him.

DAVID: What was the dream?

HENRY: Mm?

DAVID: What were you dreaming about?

Henry opens his eyes and rolls over.

HENRY: Uh … I don't really remember.

DAVID: Nothing? Place, time …

HENRY: No, I just … I don't know, I can't remember now.

DAVID: Hm. Seems strange.

HENRY: What's that.

DAVID: You just woke up.

HENRY: Yeah. Oh, right, no, yeah, that is strange, hm …

DAVID: You don't remember anything?

HENRY: I think I might have been in a field …

DAVID: So you remember some things.

HENRY: Not really. I don't know. I think it was a field. I seem to remember a lot of wide-open space.

DAVID: Right. Makes sense. Because I would think that when you first woke up would be when you remembered your dreams the most clearly. Especially if you were just having one. Do you usually remember your dreams?

Henry yawns and rolls away.

HENRY: I've been here a lot longer than you.

DAVID: I know for me, if I'm going to remember at all, it's right when I first wake up. Sometimes it's so clear it's like a picture or a film, and then gradually through the course of the day it fades until …

Well, I guess it's different for different people. So all you really know for sure is that you may or may not have been in a field.

David watches Henry.

I'll tell you what those noises sounded like, they sounded like sex noises.

HENRY: What do you want me to say, David?

DAVID: I'm just telling you –

HENRY: And I'm telling you I don't remember what my dream was.

DAVID: I'm just saying the way I interpreted –

HENRY: The dream was about you, all right? It was about you, David. You and me. We were having sex, right here in this room. I waited until you were asleep and then I made love to you and you woke up and you loved it and I loved it and we fell in love. All right?

Henry rolls away again.

The dream was about a girl, David. In a field.

And in the dream she was someone I knew. In the dream we were married. She was wearing a white dress.

We were making love. Having sex. Fucking. In a field. The sun was behind a cloud.

This fucking place. This fucking hole, and you wake me up? You wrecked it. So fuck you, and fuck off.

Henry closes his eyes. David watches him.

DAVID: So which one was it?

HENRY: I don't remember.

Blackout.

The Lesson

Lights up. Henry and David inhale deeply and speak together.

HENRY & DAVID: The board is a square

DAVID: cut into

HENRY & DAVID: sixty-four light and dark squares.

DAVID: Each square has a name:

HENRY & DAVID: a letter, A through H, and a number, One through Eight.

DAVID: All game play takes place

HENRY & DAVID: within the confines of the board.

DAVID: Two players,

HENRY & DAVID: White and Black,

DAVID: are pitted against each other. White moves

HENRY & DAVID: first;

DAVID: therefore, to begin,

HENRY & DAVID: White should play offensively, and Black, defensively.

DAVID: This can change throughout the game

HENRY & DAVID: as Initiative is lost and won. Opening game

DAVID: is the time when both players

HENRY & DAVID: attempt to control the centre. Middle game

DAVID: is the time

HENRY & DAVID: when most capturing occurs. End-game,

DAVID: loosely defined, is the time when focus turns to

HENRY & DAVID: capturing the opponent's king.

DAVID: In assigning relative value to the pieces, where a pawn equals

HENRY & DAVID: one,

DAVID: it is generally accepted that a knight equals

HENRY & DAVID: three;

DAVID: a bishop,

HENRY & DAVID: three;

DAVID: a rook,

HENRY & DAVID: five;

DAVID: and the queen,

HENRY & DAVID: nine.

DAVID: Assigning value to the king is

HENRY & DAVID: impossible;

DAVID: loss of the king equals

HENRY & DAVID: loss of the game.

DAVID: The object of the game

HENRY: is to put the enemy king

HENRY & DAVID: in checkmate,

DAVID: a position where he is

HENRY: unable to escape

HENRY & DAVID: check

HENRY: through evasion, blocking or capture.

DAVID: If the game is such that checkmate is

HENRY & DAVID: impossible,

DAVID: it is considered

HENRY & DAVID: a draw, or stalemate.

DAVID: Note: any move that causes

HENRY & DAVID: checkmate

DAVID: is considered

HENRY & DAVID: the last move of the game.

DAVID: The two kings

HENRY & DAVID: can never leave the board.

Henry looks at David.

DAVID: Good.

HENRY: And the horsey moves in an L.

DAVID: And the horsey moves in an L.
Again.

They inhale, about to speak. Blackout.

Morning Exercises

Lights up. Henry and David move together, an eccentric and completely synchronized version of tai chi. As Henry calls out the moves, their motions never cease.

HENRY: Box Tiger on Left Ear ...
Box Tiger on Right Ear ...

Repel Monkeys ...

Repel Monkeys ...

Confuse Trumpeter Swan ...

Cup Hands Like Saucers ...

Tip Your Waiter ...

Tip the Coat-Check Girl ...

Splash Water on Face ...

Elephant Never Forgets ...

Cheetah Crouches and Waits ...

Cheetah Crouches and Waits ...

Cheetah Crouches and Waits ...

Cheetah Crouches and Waits ...

Henry and David continue to crouch and wait as the lights fade to black.

God

Lights up. Henry is absently beginning the first move of Cat's Cradle with the length of rope.

DAVID: Henry, do you believe in God?

HENRY: We've done this one already.

DAVID: Have we? What did we come up with?

HENRY: Nothing useful.

David watches Henry weave the rope around his hands.

DAVID: Henry, have you ever considered the possibility that ... no one knows we're here? Or that if someone did, that they've forgotten? Or forgotten where we are?

HENRY: I've thought of that. But I don't believe that.

DAVID: Why not?

HENRY: Because that would be horrible.

Blackout.

A Big Production

Lights up. Silence. David absently makes up a song to sing to himself.

DAVID: I am sitting on the floor …
I am … leaning against the wall …
Wish that I could find the door …
Not too big and not too small.

Silence.

HENRY: (*absently, under his breath*)
I am sitting on the floor,
I am leaning against the wall,

HENRY & DAVID: (*grinning at each other*)
Wish that I could find the door,
Not too big and not too small.

Blackout.

Lights up. Henry and David are standing, trying to work something out.

HENRY: You're late on the end one.

DAVID: What?

HENRY: The end one, you're late.

DAVID: I am not late on the end one.

HENRY: Yes, you are.

DAVID: Henry –

HENRY: I'm sorry, but I've watched you every time we've done it, and –

DAVID: You're watching me?

HENRY: Yes, I'm watching you because –

DAVID: You're still upset because I didn't want to do your little –

HENRY: I am not still upset about you not liking my 'stupid' –

DAVID: I said silly, not stupid.

HENRY: I'm not upset. It's supposed to be da-da, da-da, and you're going da-da, da-da-da.

DAVID: Da-da, da-da ... You're right. Okay, let's try it again.

They regroup.

HENRY: And it wasn't stupid. Your kick idea was stupid.

David turns to Henry. Blackout.

Lights up. Big song-and-dance number, albeit with limited production values. They have obviously spent considerable time working out harmonies and choreography, including jumps, kicks and turns. The song is now lively and upbeat.

HENRY & DAVID: We are sitting on the floor,
　　　　　　　We are leaning against the wall,
　　　　　　　Wish that we could find the door,
　　　　　　　Not too big and not to small.
　　　　　　　(*etc.*)

Big finish. Blackout.

Lights up. Henry and David are sitting apart from each other. Silence.

HENRY: (*absently*) We are sitting on the –

David stands.

  Sorry.

DAVID: I will kill you.

HENRY: It was an accident.

DAVID: I am dead serious.

HENRY: It just slipped out.

DAVID: We agreed.

HENRY: Okay.

DAVID: No more.

HENRY: No more.

Blackout.

The Train

Lights up. David is lying on the floor, looking broken.

HENRY: Let's pretend we're at a train station. Let's pretend we're waiting for a train.

DAVID: Well … That's fine for now, but …

HENRY: What.

DAVID: Well … It won't come.

HENRY: It might.

DAVID: It won't.

HENRY: Didn't you ever believe in Santa Claus, David?

DAVID: He's not coming either.

HENRY: Well, the train is coming. It's just a matter of waiting.

DAVID: We're waiting anyway. All the time. All we do is wait.

HENRY: Well, now we're waiting for a train.

DAVID: Do I have to do anything?

HENRY: Nope. Just wait. Which, as you pointed out, you do anyway.

DAVID: Anything else?

HENRY: Perhaps a look of mild anticipation.

DAVID: How's this?

HENRY: Can you do any better?

DAVID: I don't think so.

HENRY: Then that's fine.

DAVID: Great, fine, I'll play your stupid game.

HENRY: Thank you.

    They wait.

DAVID: (*mumbling*) This is a stupid game.

HENRY: Hm?

DAVID: Nothing.

> *They wait.*

(*mumbling*) I feel like an idiot.

HENRY: You said something that time.

DAVID: I said I feel like an idiot. This is a stupid game.

HENRY: How do you know? We just started.

DAVID: There aren't any rules. There's no goal, nothing to strive for.

HENRY: It isn't that kind of game.

DAVID: That's the only kind there is, Henry. Rules. Goals. That's a game, that's what it is.

HENRY: Well now, obviously that isn't true. This game doesn't have those things. We just sit and wait. It's relatively easy, I don't see why you're having so much –

DAVID: All right, fine. Train, waiting, got it.

> *They wait.*

This is – I'm doing the same thing I always do, only now I feel self-conscious about it.

HENRY: Self-conscious? Really?

DAVID: Yes, very.

HENRY: Hm. Maybe that's the game.

DAVID: That's the game.

HENRY: Yes.

DAVID: To feel self-conscious.

HENRY: Maybe. It's still early on, things might change.

DAVID: I think I'm winning.

HENRY: David, I told you, it's not that kind of game.

DAVID: Yes, well, nonetheless, I feel I'm succeeding where you are not.

HENRY: This isn't winning and losing.

DAVID: Now, Henry, I think we both know that not to be the case, since I'm so clearly in the lead.

HENRY: Stop that.

DAVID: You're wasting valuable time getting angry while you could be working on feeling self-conscious.

HENRY: Stop it, I'm serious.

DAVID: So am I.

HENRY: You're changing everything.

DAVID: You said that might happen.

HENRY: What?

DAVID: You said things might change.

HENRY: Did I?

DAVID: Just a few minutes ago.

HENRY: Oh.

They wait.

Well, now I feel a bit self-conscious.

DAVID: Do you? Excellent.

HENRY: Do you still feel – ?

DAVID: Very much so.

HENRY: You don't seem like it.

DAVID: I'm compensating. I'm masking my embarrassment by trying to appear outwardly brash and overconfident. Is it working?

HENRY: It's doing something …

DAVID: (*standing*) I'm going to stand. I think this game is played better standing. You might want to do the same.

HENRY: I prefer to sit, thank you.

DAVID: Suit yourself. Just gives me an unfair advantage, is all.

They wait. Henry stands.

I don't know why we didn't do this a long time ago. So much time wasted. Oh well. Now we've got a purpose. This. This is something to do. I feel very uncomfortable, you?

HENRY: Very.

DAVID: Good, that's good.
You've really improved, I mean that.

HENRY: Is this sarcasm?

DAVID: No, no, I'm beyond sarcasm, this is something new, this is … This is waiting for a train, Henry. This is waiting for a train. That's what we're doing. Waiting.
And you know something, who's to say it isn't coming? I mean, really, I don't know, you don't know.

HENRY: No.

DAVID: Exactly. Let's take a chance. What do we have to lose? Let's just … wait and see. Deal? Is it a deal?

HENRY: Sure.

DAVID: Let's shake on it.

> *They shake hands.*

Good, I feel good about this, this train is coming, Henry. Something has to happen, why not a train? It's as good as anything else.

> *They wait. The lights grow dimmer. Henry gives up. David continues to wait.*

HENRY: I don't think it's coming.

DAVID: No.

HENRY: Sorry.

> *David continues to stand and wait.*

I'm going to get some sleep.

> *Henry finds a spot on the floor. He looks at David.*

Are you going to keep standing there like that?

DAVID: I have some things I need to think about. Personal things.

HENRY: Oh. Okay. Good night.

> *Henry curls up. David continues to stand and wait.*

You know for a while there … I really thought something was going to happen.

DAVID: Thinking personal thoughts.

HENRY: Sorry. Good night.

Blackout.

Henry's Nightmare

Lights up. Henry watches David sleep. He lies back down and closes his eyes. He begins to scream.

HENRY: No. No. No. (*etc.*)

David wakes up.

DAVID: Henry? Henry, wake up.

Henry continues. David shakes him.

Henry, wake up. Henry, it's all right, you're dreaming. Henry.

Henry continues. David cradles him.

Henry, Jesus, wake up.

Henry quiets.

Shh … You're all right now. You were having a bad dream, you're awake now. What was that all about?

HENRY: I dreamt I was alone.

They look at each other. David releases Henry and moves away from him.

DAVID: You are alone. We both are.

David crawls back to his sleeping spot and lies down.

Don't do that again. You scared the hell out of me.

HENRY: I'm sorry.

DAVID: Good night, Henry.

> *Henry curls up again. After a moment he begins to silently weep. David speaks without looking at him.*

Come on, Henry, I'm trying to sleep.

HENRY: I was just remembering something funny.

DAVID: Tell me tomorrow, all right?

HENRY: I will.

> *They try to sleep. Blackout.*

Captain Smith vs. Philidor, 1790

> *Lights up. Henry stands, looking around at different parts of the floor, trying to work something out. David waits, sitting cross-legged.*

HENRY: (*carefully*) Rook to G1.

DAVID: (*immediately*) Rook takes knight at H2: check.

HENRY: I hate you.

DAVID: Sorry.

HENRY: Don't be patronizing.

DAVID: It's your move.

HENRY: I'm thinking.

> *Henry studies the invisible pieces covering the whole floor – their 'board.'*

King takes rook at H2.

DAVID: (*immediately*) Rook to H8: check.

Henry looks over. He'd forgotten about the second rook. He extends his hand to David.

HENRY: I'd like to offer you a draw.

DAVID: Thank you, no.

HENRY: I'm offering you a draw, David.

DAVID: I have you in check, Henry.

HENRY: Does that mean you're refusing?

DAVID: Let's see your move first.

Henry attempts to take David's hand in his.

HENRY: I'm offering you a draw.

David hides his hand behind his back.

DAVID: And it's my right to see your move before I decide.

Henry looks at David. He considers the whole board carefully.

HENRY: Knight to H5.

DAVID: (*immediately*) Thank you, I decline.
Rook takes knight at H5: check.

Henry absorbs this move.

HENRY: Just remember I gave you the option.

DAVID: It's your turn.

Henry studies the board.

HENRY: King to G3.

David looks around, visualizing the board, albeit quickly.

DAVID: Knight to H3: check.

> *Henry looks from David's knight to his own king.*

HENRY: That isn't check.

DAVID: What?

HENRY: That isn't check.

DAVID: My bishop at c7.
Discovered attack.

HENRY: Discovered – ?

> *Henry looks over and falls silent. David stands and stretches, trying to crack something.*

DAVID: J'adoube.

HENRY: What?

DAVID: I adjust.

HENRY: What are you saying?

DAVID: Nothing. Pay attention. Where's my rook?

HENRY: H5.

DAVID: So?

> *Henry thinks.*

HENRY: I resign.

DAVID: Don't resign.

HENRY: I resign.

DAVID: You're only down a couple pieces.

HENRY: My development is terrible, my pawn structure's a complete mess –

DAVID: You'll never have an end-game if you keep resigning. Just play out the position.

HENRY: Are you denying me my right to resign?

DAVID: I'm not … I'm not denying you anything. I'm just suggesting that you might learn something if you play out the position. If you feel that things are so bad that your only option is to –

HENRY: Okay, Okay. Fine.

Henry studies the board.

King to G4.

DAVID: (*immediately*) Rook to H4: checkmate.

HENRY: I hate you so much.

DAVID: Sorry.

HENRY: Don't do that.

DAVID: What?

HENRY: Don't say you're sorry when you're not sorry.

DAVID: All right, I'm not sorry. I'm glad I won. I'm glad every time I win.

They stare at each other.

HENRY: Good game.

DAVID: Good game.

They do not shake hands. Blackout.

David's Choice

DAVID: This is ridiculous.

> *Lights up. Henry is in the lotus position. David is on the verge of hysterics.*

Do you hear me, Henry? This is fucking ridiculous.

HENRY: You don't have to add 'fucking' to things for me to understand.

DAVID: Well now, I don't know about that. Do you agree? That this whole thing is … fucking ridiculous?

HENRY: What?

DAVID: The whole thing. The whole thing, Henry.

HENRY: The room?

DAVID: Yes, the room. Thank you. Of course, the room.

HENRY: Well, I thought maybe you meant –

DAVID: The room, the room! Jesus, what else is there?

HENRY: I'm sorry you're upset, David.

DAVID: I have to tell you something. It isn't going to be easy for you to hear.

> I'm giving up. I'm sorry, I'm done.

> *David looks at Henry.*

Did you hear me, Henry?

HENRY: Yes.

DAVID: Yes?

HENRY: I heard you.

DAVID: Do you have anything to say about that? Anything you'd like to add?

HENRY: You should try meditating.

DAVID: I don't want to meditate.

HENRY: That's obvious. And really, in your current state I don't think you'd make much headway.

DAVID: You think I'm joking. Because I'm not huddled up in a corner rocking back and forth, crying my eyes out. This isn't a new idea, Henry, I've had time to mull this one over a bit.

HENRY: You should meditate.

DAVID: I don't want to meditate, I want a fucking cigarette.

HENRY: You're a smoker?

David considers this.

DAVID: I guess I am.

HENRY: You should quit.

DAVID: I'm sorry, what was that?

HENRY: You should quit.

DAVID: Do I have cigarettes? Do I –
      Is there a store in here somewhere that you forgot to tell me about? I think it's relatively safe to say I've quit smoking.

HENRY: If you had a cigarette right now, would you smoke it?

DAVID: Right now? If I had a cigarette right now? I'd chew it. I'd suck on the filter like a fucking dinner mint.

HENRY: Well, then you haven't quit.

DAVID: I talk to you and my head just –

HENRY: You should meditate.

David looks at Henry.

DAVID: You're trying to distract me.

HENRY: I beg your pardon?

DAVID: You're trying to lead me off-course.

HENRY: I'm not trying to do anything, David. If you feel that things are so bad that your only option is to –

DAVID: It won't work.

HENRY: I'm not trying to make it work.

DAVID: I'm sorry, Henry. And I'm sorry for how this might affect you, but I just –

HENRY: Your main problem is going to be method.

DAVID: I can't do this anymore, I –

HENRY: It's like one of those puzzle books …

DAVID: … Oh god …

HENRY: … 101 Mysteries You Can Solve …

DAVID: … I just …

HENRY: Mr. X is found dead in a dark room with no door.

DAVID: I need to think …

HENRY: The contents of the room are as follows:

DAVID: I wish I could think clearly. My head isn't clear, that's the problem ...

HENRY: One chair. One length of rope.

DAVID: I need to breathe ...

HENRY: One light fixture, hanging.

DAVID: I can't breathe ...

HENRY: Two men, Henry and David.
Did you ever read the one about the man found hanging above a puddle of water?

David thinks about this.

DAVID: Ice? Was it ice or something?

HENRY: Yes. Ice. Did you just work that out?

DAVID: Oh god ...

HENRY: You've read that before.

David screams.

DAVID: I just want to breathe air again.

HENRY: You are breathing air.

DAVID: I'm changing, aren't I. You see it, don't you.

HENRY: No.

DAVID: Look at me.

HENRY: I'm sorry. I don't know –

DAVID: Is this how it starts?

HENRY: How what starts?

DAVID: I'm getting worse.

HENRY: I don't think that's true.

DAVID: I don't care what you think. That's the truth. I don't care
what you think. You can fuck yourself, I mean that.

　　You don't think anything's wrong with me? That's because
you're already fucked. You're where I'm going.

They look away from each other.

HENRY: Maybe I could beat you to death with the chair. Maybe
that would work.

DAVID: No offence, Henry. I don't think you could beat an egg.

David softens.

I'm sorry.

HENRY: It doesn't matter.

Silence.

David? If you … give up … I'll be in this room with a corpse.

DAVID: I'm not –
　　I won't do it.

HENRY: Really?

DAVID: I wasn't really going to. I'm just tired.

David finds a place to lie down.

I'm going to sleep now. I'm very tired. I haven't been sleeping well.

HENRY: You should meditate.

David pulls himself along the floor with his hands slightly.

DAVID: Yes, I should, I should meditate.

HENRY: You'd feel better.

DAVID: I would. I really would, I should do that. I'm just going to grab a quick lie-down first.

David curls up.

HENRY: You just got up.

DAVID: I know I did, I think it was premature. I think I need more sleep. I haven't been sleeping well lately.

HENRY: You know what you should do.

DAVID: Meditate?

HENRY: Roll your pants up like a pillow.

David cradles his head between his elbows.

HENRY: Did you really just figure out that puddle thing now? I can't believe that: ice. That always stuck with me.

Blackout.

I Have Been Studying

Lights up. David is downstage facing forward. Henry is upstage with his back to us, his face turned so it is in profile.

DAVID: I have been studying how I may compare
This prison where I live unto the world;
I have passed a miserable night,
Full of fearful dreams, of ugly sights.
My thoughts are whirled like a potter's wheel:

I know not where I am, nor what I do.
I wasted time, and now doth time waste me;
For now hath time made me his numb'ring clock:
My thoughts are minutes, my dreams are seconds.
I see, as in a map, the end of all.
You common cry of curs! whose breath I hate
As reek o' th' rotten fens, whose loves I prize
As the dead carcasses of unburied men
That do corrupt my air: I banish you!
Liberty! Freedom! Tyranny is dead!
You're awfully quiet today.

HENRY: I'm actually a bit worried about you.

DAVID: When a man's verses cannot be understood, nor a man's
good wit seconded with the forward child, understanding, it
strikes a man more dead than a great reckoning in a little room.
Truly, Henry, I would the gods had made thee poetical.

HENRY: Are we in trouble, David?

DAVID: All is not well.

HENRY: What's happening?

DAVID: Ask me not what I know.
Between the acting of a dreadful thing
And the first motion, all the interim is
Like a phantasma, or a hideous dream:

HENRY: David –

DAVID: We will proceed no further in this business.
Nothing will come of nothing.
There is a world elsewhere.

Blackout.

What Is Important Is What Is

Lights up. David is manic. Henry watches him.

DAVID: What is important is what is –
What is –
What is important is what is … good and what is true. No, what –
The important thing –
The important thing is, is what is –
I'm asking myself the wrong questions: Why, how. What if someone told me? What if someone just –

David laughs.

Just walked up and told me: this. Because of this and this way. And then left.

David laughs.

And then left. Then what? I'd be no better off.
What is important –
No, what is –
No, the important thing is to … uncover … what is true. This place. If this were in a story it would have to mean something. But we can't assume –
This room, this inanimate –
This room doesn't know what it's doing, it's just a, a collection of basic –
In, in combination with –
Built by random –
Or people, maybe, I mean, likely someone –
Well, no, no, that's not –
Wrong. Dead wrong. This room does not know what it is doing to us. This is not your fault.

HENRY: My fault.

DAVID: You don't know what you're doing.

HENRY: Are you talking to me, David?

DAVID: Why? No, again, I can't help it. I need –

I need –

I don't know, something's, I can't –

I'm sorry. I'm sorry, I can't do this anymore, I'm trying so hard, but –

It isn't going away. I thought it would go away but it isn't –

HENRY: David –

DAVID: No. No. No. No. No. No. No. This can't be what happens, this isn't right. We had so much time. We had so much time and we squandered it, didn't we? On games.

Am I being punished? Is that what this is? Did I fail some fucking test? Well, I don't accept that. I do not accept that. The problem –

The problem is that we have no frame of –

No high water –

No, no litmus –

No standard by which to measure … truth. That word. I'm not comfortable with that word. We need a, a lie detector. To measure the truth. That's what we need. Did you –

Did you remember to bring your lie detector, Henry?

HENRY: No. Sorry. I forgot it.

DAVID: Did you?

David laughs.

In your other pants? That's too bad. That's good, though, I like that.

HENRY: That's a David joke.

DAVID: A what? A what?

HENRY: I just –

DAVID: That's what we need. A lie detector, something to monitor what is being said, and by whom. Records have to be kept if we hope to, to …

HENRY: To what?

DAVID: Lies have been told. In this very room. Lies have been told. You have lied.

HENRY: I have.

DAVID: Yes. You told me you were in charge.

HENRY: That was a long time ago. And I never said that.

DAVID: You led me to believe. Of course, you were frightened.

HENRY: I am frightened.

DAVID: And why shouldn't you be? Why shouldn't you be.

HENRY: Why didn't you kill me? Or at least tie me to the chair.

DAVID: I'm not like you.

HENRY: What?

DAVID: I too have lied.

HENRY: You lied.

DAVID: I lied. Because what is here to prevent it. And because maybe something that would otherwise not happen …
   So yes, I lied. I lied. There.

HENRY: About what?

DAVID: Everything. I told you that I loved the ocean. I do not love the ocean. I've never even seen the ocean. Except in pictures, and even the pictures I did not love.

HENRY: You told me –

DAVID: I told you that I smoked, when in fact, I have never smoked a day in my life. The fact is, and I feel very strongly about this, it disgusts me.
I, I told you … my name …

HENRY: Your name. It isn't David.

DAVID: I had to keep you off balance, any edge I could get. You never give your real name in these situations, Henry. That's, that's the first thing they teach you when, when, when you're out of the gate.

HENRY: What is your name? Your real name.

DAVID: My real name?

HENRY: Yes.

DAVID: I don't know. And I'll tell you something else: I don't think you know yours either.

HENRY: It's Henry.

DAVID: Grow up.

HENRY: What else. Is that it? Is that everything?

DAVID: No, I told you: everything, I lied about everything. I told you that I, I played chess, I don't play chess, I've never played chess, I don't know how.

HENRY: You taught me.

DAVID: I made it up.

HENRY: We played games –

DAVID: (*overlapping*) I wanted to feel superior.

HENRY: … in our heads.

DAVID: I made it all up.

Henry looks at David.

HENRY: King's pawn to E4.

DAVID: (*automatically*) Pawn to C5: Sicilian Defence, famous, classic opening, it doesn't matter. It's gibberish, I made it up.

HENRY: I don't believe you.

DAVID: We should have starved to death. We should have shit ourselves.

HENRY: We played entire games.

DAVID: We should have fallen asleep and never woken up.

HENRY: It all worked.

DAVID: Did it?

HENRY: Yes. Perfectly.

David considers this.

DAVID: Then maybe it's the room. Maybe –
Listen, perhaps this room itself is a, uh, a, uh …
So that in, in a way we're creating our own, our own –
So that I can't, I can't remember my name, my real name.

I've forgotten what it was. But because it no longer is, my only real name is and always has been what it is right now. This very moment.

HENRY: David.

DAVID: Maybe that's what's important. So that the –
Not outside, as something dictated by a, a, by some third party, but within. To come out of our bodies as sure, and, and as real as breath. This is something that we form, we are creating –
No. We … are …
The truth is: we aren't eating because we choose not to be hungry. We aren't shitting because we choose not to eat. We aren't sleeping because we choose not to dream.

HENRY: I only pretended to sleep.

DAVID: The truth … The truth is that we are here, and that we will remain here … Until we choose to leave.

HENRY: I want to leave.

DAVID: No, see, that's the interesting part. You don't.

HENRY: Yes. I do.

DAVID: Then say it.

HENRY: I want to leave.

DAVID: Not what you want. Just say it. Say that you're free.

They look at each other.

HENRY: You're free.

David looks at Henry in surprise. He looks over at the downstage wall and sees something. He walks toward it in a slow, dreamlike

state. He stops at the edge of the floor and extends his hands out …
and through the wall. His eyes grow wide. A look of worry crosses
his face. He pulls his hands back inside and staggers back, confused.

DAVID: Why are you doing this?

David reacts as if punched in the stomach, collapsing backward onto
the floor.

I just … I want to go back … I want to go back …
What's happening to me?

HENRY: I don't know, I think you're sick.

DAVID: I'm sorry … I'm so sorry …

HENRY: David –

DAVID: What is important is what is …

HENRY: You're tired. You should rest for a while.

David crawls to Henry on his hands and knees as he speaks. He
convulses occasionally without seeming to notice.

DAVID: So I –
Don't I –
Sometimes I –
Sometimes I feel –
And sometimes –
Remember –

HENRY: You need to rest, David.

David puts his head in Henry's lap, like a child.

DAVID: I –

David convulses one last time and stares out vacantly. Blackout.

Epilogue

Lights up. The distant sound of waves crashing against rocks. David is still fetal, his head on Henry's lap, staring out vacantly.

HENRY: I can hear you breathing. I like listening to you breathe.

Henry looks out, as though watching the ocean.

You know that thing where the wall meets the floor? That looks like something but turns out to be nothing? It just showed up one day.

I remember when it first appeared. Big excitement back then. I spent a lot of time picturing that little ... something ... Travelling up, and over, and down, and cracking ... Or spreading out like red wine on a tablecloth ... Filling out the shape of a door ... The shadow of a door becoming a door ... And opening ... Light flooding in like those pictures of God. Walking out into ...

What would you do first?

Henry looks down at David, who continues to stare out vacantly. He looks back up.

I wished for that. All the strength I had, and it never ... So after a while, I stopped. I made a choice. I changed the way I thought about things. And then you were here.

Are you listening? I think I brought you here. I don't know how.

And there's more. Are you listening? This place.

I'm starting to think ... I built it. Isn't that strange? I don't remember doing it, but ...

And I'm sorry. I'm sorry if I did that. But I'm glad too. I'm glad you're here. I don't know what I'd do without you.

Henry looks down at David, then back up.

I wish I had your strength, I really do.

They watch the ocean.

I've been thinking about that story I told you. About the tortoise? I've changed it around a bit. Would you like to hear?

David says nothing.

Once, there was a boy who had a tortoise and no one else.

The boy was small, but the tortoise was smaller, so the boy promised to always look after him.

And even though the boy was a boy and the tortoise was in fact a tortoise, they became fast friends.

One day, as they sat in the sun watching the water, the boy said to the tortoise, I love it here. It's so quiet. Sometimes I think this is my favourite place.

The tortoise smiled.

Henry looks down at David, then back up, smiling.

You're quiet today.

The sound of waves crashing against rocks fades up as the lights fades to black.

About the Author

Brendan Gall is the author of four plays: *A Quiet Place*, *Panhandled*, *Alias Godot* and *Wide Awake Hearts*. In addition, he has co-written or co-created eight other works for companies such as Public Recordings, Unspun Theatre, Convergence Theatre and Small Wooden Shoe. His writing has been nominated for three Dora Mavor Moore awards, translated into Italian and produced in the United States and Italy. His screenplay for the feature film *Dakota*, distributed by Mongrel Media, won the Special Jury Prize at the Winnipeg Film Festival. Brendan is one of the founders and artistic directors of Toronto-based creation company The Room, and is currently a playwright-in-residence at Tarragon Theatre. He is also an actor.

Typeset in Adobe Jenson
Printed and bound at the Coach House at 80 bpNichol Lane,
October 2010

Edited and designed by Alana Wilcox
Cover art by Tyler Vincent Shields, courtesy of the artist
Author photo by Ian Brown (ianbrownphotography.com)

DATE DUE	RETURNED
SEP 2 6 2012	SEP 2 1 2012

Coach H
80 bpNi
Toronto

416 979
800 367

mail@ch
www.chl